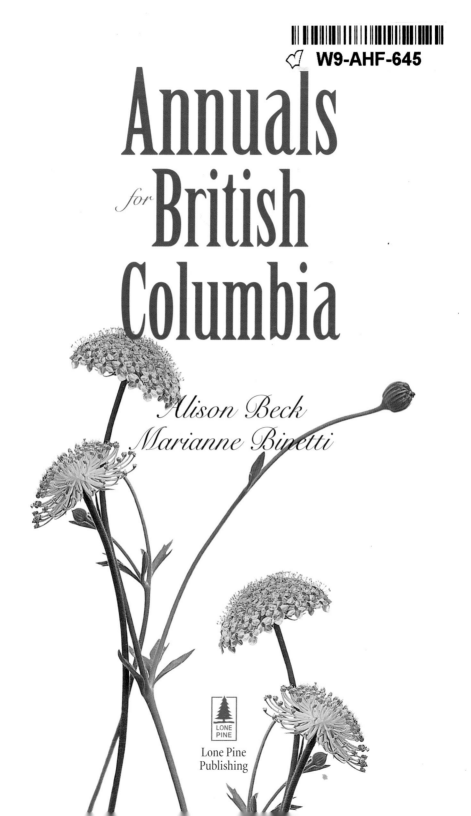

Annuals *for* British Columbia

Alison Beck
Marianne Binetti

LONE
PINE

Lone Pine
Publishing

The Publisher: Lone Pine Publishing

10145 – 81 Ave.	202A, 1110 Seymour St.	1901 Raymond Ave. SW,
Edmonton, AB T6E 1W9	Vancouver, BC V6B 3N3	Suite C, Renton, WA 98055
Canada	Canada	USA

Website: http://www.lonepinepublishing.com

Canadian Cataloguing in Publication Data

Beck, Alison
  Annuals for British Columbia

  Includes index.
  ISBN 1-55105-156-7

  1. Annuals (Plants)--British Columbia. 2. Gardening--British Columbia.
  I. Binetti, Marianne, 1956- II. Title.
  SB422.B42 2000   635.9'312'09711   C00-910108-X

Editorial Director: Nancy Foulds
Project Editor: Erin McCloskey
Editorial: Erin McCloskey, Lee Craig
Production Manager: Jody Reekie
Book Design: Heather Markham
Cover Design: Rob Weidemann
Layout & Production: Heather Markham
Image Editing: Curt Pillipow, Elliot Engley
Scanning, Separations & Film: Elite Lithographers Company

Photography: all photographs are by Tim Matheson, except Therese D'Monte 5s, 6d, 124, 135b, 146, 147a, 148b; Elliot Engley 23b, 24, 25a, 25b; EuroAmerican 6m, 7s, 57b, 57c, 129a, 130a, 138, 139a, 171c, 174b, 175; Anne Gordon 4f, 5j, 6t, 7j, 52, 53b, 89c, 101a, 112, 113b, 192a, 201, 216; Al Harvey 242b; Horticultural Photography 4t, 5a, 5b, 5e, 5p, 6l, 7l, 17a, 56, 57a, 75b, 79b, 88, 90, 91a, 91b, 92, 93a, 93b, 101b, 126, 127a, 127b, 129b, 131, 139b, 143b, 168, 169, 183b, 192b, 193a, 193b, 200, 220, 221a, 221b; David McDonald 4c, 5i, 6n, 50b, 51a, 86, 87a, 87b, 110, 172, 173b, 191b, 243; Joy Spurr 4j, 4n, 4o, 5g, 5h, 6b, 6i, 7a, 7c, 7k, 7t, 7c, 14, 17, 27, 28a, 36, 65b, 68, 69, 76, 78, 79a, 89b, 106, 107a, 107b, 108, 111, 113a, 139a, 142, 148c, 158, 159b, 173c, 191a, 195a, 195b, 198, 199, 219b, 241b; Peter Thompstone 50a, 51b, 77a, 77b, 109a, 109b, 123b, 147b, 149a, 159a, 170, 171a, 171b, 189a, 217a, 217b, 241a, 242a

Cover Photographs by Tim Matheson

We acknowledge the financial support of the Government of Canada through the Book Publishing Industry Development Program (BPIDP) for our publishing activities.

PC: 4

Contents

Acknowledgments

We would like to express our appreciation to all who were involved in the making of this project. Special thanks are extended to the following organizations: in Vancouver, BC, to Acadia Community Garden, UBC, Compost Demonstration Garden, Maple Leaf Nurseries, Murray Nurseries, Park and Tilford Gardens, Queen Elizabeth Park, Southlands Nursery, Southside Perennials, Stanley Park, UBC Botanical Garden, Van Dusen Gardens, West Van Florist; in Victoria, BC, to Butchart Gardens; in Rosedale to Minter Gardens. Additional thanks to Peter Thompstone and Christine Savage for their involvement in preparing this book.

Pictorial Index
Alphabetical Order, by Common Name

African Daisy
p. 42

Ageratum
p. 44

Amaranth
p. 48

Baby's Breath
p. 52

Bachelor's Buttons
p. 54

Bacopa
p. 56

Begonia
p. 58

Bells-of-Ireland
p. 62

Black-eyed Susan
p. 64

Black-eyed Susan
Vine, p. 68

Blanket Flower
p. 70

Blue Lace Flower
p. 72

Blue Marguerite
p. 74

Browallia
p. 76

Butterfly Flower
p. 78

Calendula
p. 80

California Poppy
p. 82

Candytuft
p. 84

Canterbury Bells
p. 86

Cape Marigold
p. 88

China Aster
p. 90

Chrysanthemum
p. 92

Cockscomb
p. 94

Coleus
p. 96

Coreopsis
p. 100

Cosmos
p. 102

Creeping Zinnia
p. 106

Cup Flower
p. 108

Cup-and-saucer Vine
p. 110

Dahlberg Daisy
p. 112

Dahlia
p. 114

Dusty Miller
p. 118

Dwarf Morning Glory,
p. 120

Fan Flower
p. 122

Forget-me-not
p. 124

Four-o'clock Flower
p. 126

Fuchsia
p. 128

Gazania
p. 132

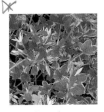

Geranium
p. 134

Gerbera Daisy
p. 138

Globe Amaranth
p. 140

Godetia
p. 142

Heliotrope
p. 144

Impatiens
p. 146

Licorice Plant
p. 150

Livingstone Daisy
p. 152

Lobelia
p. 154

Love-in-a-mist
p. 156

Madagascar
Periwinkle, p. 158

Mallow
p. 160

Marigold
p. 164

Mexican Sunflower
p. 168

Million Bells
p. 170

Morning Glory
p. 172

Nasturtium
p. 176

Nicotiana
p. 180

Painted-tongue
p. 182

Petunia
p. 184

Phlox
p. 188

Poppy
p. 190

Portulaca
p. 194

Prairie Gentian
p. 196

Prickly Poppy
p. 198

Rocket Larkspur
p. 200

Salvia
p. 202

Scabiosa
p. 206

Snapdragon
p. 208

Spider Flower
p. 212

Statice
p. 214

Stock
p. 216

Strawflower
p. 218

Summer forget-
me-not, p. 220

Sunflower
p. 222

Swan River Daisy
p. 226

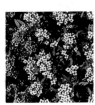

Sweet Alyssum
p. 228

Sweet Pea
p. 230

Verbena
p. 232

Viola
p. 234

Wishbone Flower
p. 238

Zinnia
p. 240

Introduction

*A*nnuals are plants that complete their full life cycle in one growing season. Within one year they germinate, mature, bloom, set seed and die. Annuals are sometimes referred to as bedding plants because they are used to provide color and fill in garden beds. Most annuals are started indoors and then transplanted into the garden after the last spring frost, but some can be sown directly in the garden. A sure sign of spring's arrival is the rush of gardeners to local garden centers, greenhouses and farmers' markets to pick out their new annuals.

British Columbia has wonderful climates for growing annuals. While the heat has annuals in some parts of the country fading by August, annuals like lobelia, fuchsia and begonia are still going strong on the coast. The weather is cool and damp in the spring and warm and dry in late summer and fall. Gardeners in Victoria pride themselves on having Canada's first spring flowers; and in Vancouver, some people grow fig and palm trees quite successfully with winter frost protection. The interior of B.C. is pocketed with warm, dry valleys with a relatively shorter growing season. Here, sun-loving, drought-tolerant annuals, like marigold, nasturtium and portulaca, welcome summer with waves of color. The Okanagan Valley and the Thompson–Okanagan region tend to be hot in summer and cold in winter. It is drier than the coast, with parts that are even desert-like, requiring irrigation for the bountiful fruit orchards. The northern regions and higher altitudes, such as in the Kootenays and the Cariboo-Chilcotin, face a short growing season, when cold weather or even snow may occur on almost any day. Frost-tolerant, fast-growing annuals, like calendula, candytuft and godetia, are undaunted by these conditions.

Annuals are popular because they produce lots of flowers, in a wide variety of colors, over a long period of time. Many annuals bloom continuously from spring right through until early fall. Beyond this basic appeal gardeners are constantly finding new ways to include annuals in their gardens, using them to accent areas in an established border or as the main attraction in a new garden, or combining them with trees or shrubs, perennials and even vegetables. Many annuals are adapted to a variety of growing conditions, from hot, dry sun to cool, damp shade. Because annuals are temporary and inexpensive, they are fun for beginner or adventurous gardeners and can be easily replaced if they are undesirable or past their prime.

There are popular annuals that many gardeners grow every year, but there are always new varieties and new species to try. Some of the most popular, easy to grow and reliable annuals include geraniums, petunias, pansies, impatiens and marigolds.

In recent years, gardeners have also developed an interest in unusual varieties. Some beautiful annuals that have been overlooked in the past because they bloom late are now in wider use. New species have been introduced from other parts of the world. There are new and sometimes improved varieties of old favorites with an expanded color range or increased pest resistance. The use of heritage varieties has been revived partly owing to concerns with over-hybridization and interests in organic gardening. The selection of annuals is increasing every year.

When new varieties are introduced, some may experience a short period of popularity but are soon forgotten. Greatly improved varieties that have been tried in gardens across the United States and Canada may be judged by members of the horticultural industry to become 'All-American Selections Winners.' These outstanding plants are most widely known and frequently grown.

Average Last Spring Frost Dates

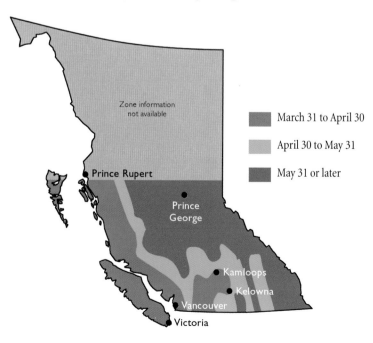

Zone information not available

■ March 31 to April 30

■ April 30 to May 31

■ May 31 or later

Prince Rupert

Prince George

Kamloops

Kelowna

Vancouver

Victoria

Annual Gardens

*A*nnuals are often used in combination with perennials, shrubs and trees. Because these plants bloom at different times during the growing season, including a variety of annuals in the garden provides continuous color. Annuals are also perfect for filling in bare spaces around small or leggy shrubs or between perennials that sprout late in the season. Include annuals anywhere that you would like some variety and an extra splash of color—in pots staggered up porch steps or on a deck, in windowsill planters or in hanging baskets. Even well-established gardens are brightened with the addition of annual flowers.

The short life of annuals allow gardeners a large degree of flexibility and freedom when planning a garden. Where trees and shrubs form the permanent structure or the bones of the garden, and perennials and groundcovers fill the spaces between them, annuals add bold patterns and bright splashes of color. Annuals give gardeners the opportunity to make the same garden look different each year. Even something as simple as a planting of impatiens under a tree can be different each year with different varieties and color combinations. When planning your garden, find as many sources as you can. Look through gardening books and ask friends and greenhouse

Informal border

When choosing annuals most people make the color, size and shape of the flowers their prime consideration. Other things to consider are the size and shape of the plant. Annual foliage plants are attractive, particularly when used in mixed hanging baskets and planters. A variety of flower and plant sizes, shapes and colors will make your garden more interesting. Consult the Quick Reference Chart on p. 244.

Colors have different effects on our senses. Cool colors such as purple, blue and green are soothing and can make a small garden appear larger. Some annuals with cool colors are lobelia, ageratum and browallia. If you have a hectic life and need to relax when you are at home, then sitting in a garden of cool-colored flowers will help. Warm colors such as red, orange and yellow are more stimulating and appear to fill larger spaces. Warm colors can make even the largest most imposing garden seem warm and welcoming. Some annuals with warm colors are salvia, calendula and cockscomb.

experts for advice. Notice what you like or dislike about various gardens, and make a list of the plants you would like to include in your garden.

There are many styles of gardens, and annuals can be used in any of them. A tidy, symmetrical, formal garden can be enhanced by adding only a few types of annuals or by picking annuals that are all the same color. You may want to add a dash of the informal to the same garden by adding many different species and colors of annuals to relax the neat plantings of trees and shrubs. An in-formal, cottage-style garden can be a riot of plants and colors. The same garden will look less chaotic and even soothing if you use several species that bloom in cool shades of blue and purple. Whatever style you want your garden to have can be cleverly created by mixing annuals.

If you work long hours and only have time to enjoy your garden in the evenings, you may want to consider pale colors like white and yellow. These show up well at dusk and even at night. Some plants have flowers that only open in the evenings and often have fragrant blossoms that add an attractive dimension to the evening garden. Moonflower is a twining vine-like plant whose large, white, fragrant flowers open when the sun sets.

Foliage color varies a great deal as well. There are annuals that are grown for the interesting or colorful foliage and not for the flowers at all, yet some plants have both interesting foliage and flowers. Leaves can be in any shade of green and may be covered in a soft white down or they can be so dark they almost appear black. Some foliage is patterned or has veins that contrast with the color of the leaves. Foliage plants like coleus are often used by themselves while others like dusty miller provide an interesting backdrop against brightly colored flowers.

Coleus

Swan River Daisy

ANNUALS WITH INTERESTING FOLIAGE

Amaranth 'Illumination'
Begonia
Coleus
Dusty Miller
Licorice Plant
Nasturtium
Sweet Potato Vine

FINE-TEXTURED ANNUALS

Bacopa
Dahlberg Daisy
Lobelia
Swan River Daisy
Sweet Alyssum

Texture is another element of planning a garden. Both flowers and foliage have a visual texture. Larger leaves can appear coarse in texture, and they can make a garden appear smaller and more shaded. Coarse-textured flowers appear bold and dramatic and can be seen from farther away. Small leaves appear fine in texture, and these create a sense of increased space and light. Fine-textured flowers appear soothing and even a little mysterious. Sometimes the flowers and foliage of a plant have contrasting textures. Using a variety of textures is interesting and appealing in the garden.

COARSE-TEXTURED ANNUALS

Dahlia (large flowered)
Chrysanthemum
Sunflower
Sweet Potato Vine
Zinnia

Sunflower

Getting Started

*F*inding the right annuals for your garden is a process of experimentation and creativity. Before you start planting, coordinate the growing conditions in your garden with the needs of specific plants. This will influence not only the types of plants that you select, but also the locations in which you plant them. The plants will be healthier and less susceptible to problems if grown in optimum conditions. It is difficult to significantly modify your garden's existing conditions; an easier approach is to match the plants to the garden.

The porosity, pH and texture of soil, the levels of light and the amount of exposure in your garden provide guidelines for your plant selection. Sketching your garden helps to visualize how various conditions might affect your planting decisions. Note shaded areas, low-lying or wet areas, exposed or windy sections, etc. Understanding your garden's growing conditions can help you learn to recognize which plants will perform best, and it can prevent you from making costly mistakes in your planting decisions. Consult the Quick Reference Chart on p.244.

Soil

Soil quality is an extremely important element of a healthy garden. Plant roots rely on the air, water and nutrients that are held within soil. Of course, plants also depend on soil to hold them upright. The soil in turn benefits from plant roots breaking down large soil particles. Plants prevent soil erosion by binding together small particles and reducing the amount of exposed surface. When plants die and break down they add organic nutrients to soil and feed beneficial micro-organisms.

Soil is made up of particles of different sizes. Sand particles are the largest, water drains quickly from sandy soil and nutrients tend to get washed away. Sandy soil does not compact very easily, because the large particles leave air pockets between them. Clay particles, which are the smallest, can only be seen through a microscope. Clay holds the most nutrients, but it also compacts easily and has little air space. Clay is slow to absorb water and equally slow to let it drain. Most soils are composed of a combination of different particle sizes and are called loams.

It is important to consider the pH level (the scale on which the acidity or alkalinity is measured) of soil, which influences the availability of nutrients. Most plants thrive in soil with a pH between 5.5 and 7.5. In the Pacific Northwest most soils are quite acidic. Testing kits can be purchased at most garden centers. There are also soil testing labs that can fully analyze the pH as well as the quantities of various nutrients in your soil. The acidity of soil can be reduced with the use of horticultural lime or the addition of wood ashes. For plants that prefer a very alkaline soil, you might wish to use planters or create raised beds where it is easier to control and alter the pH level of soil.

Water drainage is affected by soil type and terrain in your garden. Plants that prefer well-drained soil and do not require a large amount of moisture grow well on a sloping hillside garden with rocky soil. Water retention in these areas will be improved through the addition of organic matter. Whereas plants that thrive on a consistent water supply or boggy conditions are ideal for low-lying areas that retain water for longer periods or hardly drain at all. In extremely wet areas, you can improve drainage with the addition of sand or gravel or by creating raised beds.

ANNUALS FOR MOIST SOIL

Spider Flower
Forget-me-not
Wishbone Flower
Pansy
Mallow

ANNUALS FOR DRY SOIL

Cape Marigold
Coreopsis
Cosmos
Portulaca
Marigold

Light

There are four categories of light that affect a garden: full sun, partial shade, light shade and full shade. Available light is affected by buildings, trees, fences and the position of the sun at different times of the day. Knowing what light is available in your garden will help you determine where to place each plant.

Plants in full-sun locations, such as along south-facing walls, receive direct sunlight for all or most of the day. Locations classified as partial sun or partial shade, such as east- or west-facing walls, receive direct sunlight for part of the day and shade for the rest. Light-shade locations receive shade for most or all of the day, although some sunlight does filter through to ground level. An example of a light-shade location might be the ground under a small-leaved tree such as a birch. Full-shade locations, which would include the north side of a house, receive no direct sunlight.

Plant your annuals where they will grow best. For hot and dry areas, for low-lying, damp sections of the garden, select plants that prefer those conditions. Experimenting with annuals will help you learn about the conditions of your garden.

Sun-loving plants may become tall and straggly and flower poorly in too much shade. Shade-loving plants may get scorched leaves or even wilt and die if they get too much sun. Many plants are tolerant of a wide range of light conditions.

ANNUALS FOR SUN
Amaranth
Cockscomb
Cosmos
Geranium
Heliotrope
Marigold
Portulaca
Spider Flower
Statice

ANNUALS FOR SHADE
Browallia
Busy Lizzie Impatiens
Canterbury Bells
Forget-me-not
Godetia
Nicotiana
Pansy
Tuberous Begonia

ANNUALS FOR ANY LIGHT
Black-eyed Susan
Black-eyed Susan Vine
Coleus
Cup Flower
Fan Flower
Licorice Vine
Lobelia
Nasturtium
New Guinea Impatiens
Wax Begonia

Cosmos

Exposure

Wind, heat, cold and rain are the elements your garden is exposed to and some plants are better adapted to withstand the potential damage of these forces. Buildings, walls, fences, hills, hedges, trees and even tall plants influence and often reduce exposure.

Wind and heat are the most likely to cause damage to annuals. The sun can be very intense and heat can rise quickly on a sunny afternoon. Plant annuals that tolerate or even thrive in hot weather in the hot-spots in your garden.

Over-watering or too much rain can be damaging. Early in the season, seed or seedlings can be washed away in heavy rain. Mulch will help prevent this problem. Established annuals (or their flowers) can be beaten down by heavy rain. Most annuals will recover, but some, like petunias, are slow to do so. Choose plants or varieties that are quick to recover from rain damage. Many of the small-flowered petunia varieties now available are quick to recover from heavy rain.

Hanging moss-lined baskets are susceptible to wind and heat exposure losing water from the soil surface and the leaves. Water can evaporate from all sides of a moss basket, and in hot or windy locations moisture can be depleted very quickly. Such baskets look wonderful, but watch for wilting and water the baskets regularly to keep them looking great.

Mulching a bed prevents soil erosion.

A hanging basket requires frequent watering.

Frost Tolerance

When planting annuals, consider their tolerance to an unexpected frost. The last frost date and first frost date varies greatly from region to region in North America. In the Pacific Northwest, coastal gardens may have a last frost in March while gardens in the mountains may have a last frost date in early June. The map on page 10 gives a general idea of when you can expect your last frost date. Keep in mind that these dates can vary greatly from year to year and within the general regions. Your local garden center should be able to provide information on frost expectations in your area.

Annuals are grouped into three categories based on how tolerant they are of cold weather: they are either hardy, half-hardy or tender. Consult the Quick Reference Chart on p. 244.

Hardy annuals can tolerate low temperatures and even frost. They can be planted in the garden early and may continue to flower long into fall or even winter. I had hardy calendulas planted close to the house and they continued to flower even after a snowfall covered them. Many hardy annuals are sown directly in the garden before the last frost date.

Half-hardy annuals can tolerate a light frost but will be killed by a heavy one. These annuals can be planted out around the last frost date and will generally benefit from being started early from seed indoors.

Tender annuals have no frost tolerance at all and might even suffer if the temperatures drop to a few degrees above freezing. These plants are often started early and not planted in the garden until the last frost date has passed and the ground has had a chance to warm up. The upside to these annuals is that they are often tolerant of hot summer temperatures.

Protecting plants from frost is relatively simple. Plants can be covered overnight with sheets, towels, burlap or even cardboard boxes. Refrain from using plastic because it doesn't retain heat and therefore doesn't provide plants with any insulation.

Calendula

Preparing the Garden

*T*aking the time to properly pre- pare your flowerbeds before you plant out will save you time and effort over summer. Starting out with as few weeds as possible and with well prepared soil that has had organic material added will give your annuals a good start. For container gardens, use potting soil because regular garden soil loses its structure, quickly compacting into a solid mass that drains poorly when used in pots. Many gardening problems can be avoided with good preparation and maintenance.

Loosen the soil with a large garden fork and remove the weeds. Avoid working the soil when it is very wet or very dry because you will damage the soil structure by breaking down the pockets that hold air and water. Add organic matter and work it into the soil with a spade or rototiller.

Organic matter is a small but impor- tant component of soil. It increases the water holding and nutrient hold- ing capacity of sandy soil and binds together the large particles. In a clay soil organic matter will increase the water absorbing and draining poten- tial by opening up spaces between the tiny particles. Common organic additives for your soil are things like grass clippings, shredded leaves, peat moss, chopped straw, well-rotted manure or composted hemlock bark.

Compost worms

Wooden compost bins

Plastic compost bins

Composting

Any organic matter you add will be of greater benefit to your soil if it has been composted first. Adding organic matter to soil not only improves soil structure, it also adds nutrients.

In natural environments, such as forests or meadows, compost is created when leaves, plant bits and other debris are broken down on the soil surface. This process will also take place in your garden beds by working fresh organic matter into the soil. However, micro-organisms that break organic matter down use the same nutrients as your plants. The tougher the organic matter the more nutrients in the soil will be used up trying to break it the matter down. This will rob your plants of vital nutrients, particularly nitrogen. Also, fresh organic matter and garden debris might encourage or introduce pests and diseases in your garden.

It is best to compost organic matter before adding it to your garden beds, because it must break down and decompose before your plants can use the nutrients. A compost pile or bin, which can be built or purchased, creates a controlled environment where organic matter can be fully broken down before being introduced to your garden. Good composting methods also reduce the possibility of spreading pests and diseases.

Creating compost is a simple process. Kitchen scraps, grass clippings and fall leaves will slowly break down if left in a pile. The process can be sped up by following a few simple guidelines.

Your compost pile should contain both dry and fresh materials, with a larger proportion of dry matter such as chopped straw, shredded leaves or sawdust. Fresh green matter, such as vegetable scraps, grass clippings or pulled weeds, breaks down quickly and produces nitrogen, which feeds the decomposer organisms while they break down the tougher dry matter.

Layer the green matter with the dry matter and mix in small amounts of soil from your garden or previously finished compost. The addition of

Composting materials   Hot compost decomposing   Finished compost

soil or compost will introduce beneficial micro-organisms. If the pile seems very dry, sprinkle some water between the layers—the compost should be moist but not soaking wet. Adding nitrogen, like that found in fertilizer, will speed up decomposition. Avoid strong concentrations that can kill beneficial organisms.

Each week or two, use a pitchfork to turn the pile over or poke holes into it. This will help aerate the material, which will speed up decomposition. A compost pile that is kept aerated can generate a lot of heat. Temperatures can reach up to 160° F (71° C). Such a high temperature will destroy weed seeds and kill many damaging organisms. Most beneficial organisms will not be killed unless the temperature rises higher than this. To monitor the temperature of the compost near the middle of the pile you will need a thermometer that is attached to a long probe, like a large version of a meat thermometer. Turn your compost once the temperature drops. Turning and aerating the pile will stimulate the process to heat up again. The pile can be left

to sit; the pile will be ready to use without turning if you are willing to wait several months.

Avoid adding diseased or pest-ridden materials to your compost pile. If the damaging organisms are not destroyed they could be spread throughout your garden. If you do add material you suspect of harboring pests or diseases, add it near the center of the pile where the temperature is highest.

When you can no longer recognize the matter that you put into the compost bin, and the temperature no longer rises upon turning, your compost is ready to be mixed into your garden beds. This process can take as little as one month and will leave you with organic material that is rich in nutrients and beneficial organisms.

Compost can be purchased from most garden centers. Add a trowelful of compost to the planting hole and mix it into the garden soil before adding your annual.

Selecting Annuals

rewarding aspects of gardening. There are benefits to both methods and many gardeners choose to use a combination of the two. Purchasing plants provides you with plants that are well grown and often already in bloom, which is useful if you don't have the room or the facilities to start seeds. Some seeds require specific conditions that are difficult to achieve in a house or have erratic germination rates that make them impractical. Starting from seed may offer you a greater selection of species and varieties listed in seed catalogs than at garden centers. How to start annuals from seed is discussed on p.24.

Purchased annual plants are grown in a variety of different containers. Some are sold in individual pots, some in divided cell-packs and others in undivided trays. There are positive and negative aspects to each method.

Annuals in individual pots are usually well established and have plenty of space for root growth. Annuals have probably been seeded in flat trays and then transplanted into individual pots once they developed a few leaves. The cost of labor, pots and soil can make these more expensive options. If you are planting a large area you may also find it difficult to transport large numbers of plants.

Annuals grown in cell-packs are often inexpensive and hold several plants making them easy to transport.

*M*any gardeners consider the trip to the local garden center to pick out their annual plants an important right of spring. Other gardeners consider starting their own annuals from seed to be one of the most

There is less damage to the roots of the plants when they are transplanted, but because each cell is quite small it doesn't take too long for the plant to become root-bound.

Annuals grown in undivided trays have plenty of room for root growth and can be left in the trays for longer that other types of containers, however, their roots tend to become entangled making the plants difficult to separate.

Lobelia

Regardless of the type of container, the best plants to choose are often not yet flowering. These plants are younger and are unlikely to be root-bound. Check for roots emerging from the holes at the bottom of the cells or gently remove the plant from the container to look at the roots. In either case, too many roots means that the plant is too mature for the container, especially if the roots are wrapped around the inside of the container in a thick web. Such plants are slow to establish once they are transplanted into the garden.

The plants should be compact and have good color. Healthy leaves look firm and vibrant. Unhealthy leaves may be wilted, chewed or discolored. Tall, leggy plants have likely been deprived of light. Sickly plants may not survive being transplanted and may spread pests or diseases to the rest of your garden.

Once you get your annuals home, water them if they are dry. Annuals growing in small containers may require water more than once a day.

Begin to harden off the plants so they can be transplanted into the garden as soon as possible. Your annuals are probably accustomed to growing in the sheltered environment of a greenhouse, and they will need to become accustomed to the climate outdoors. They can be placed outdoors in a lightly shaded spot each day and brought into a sheltered porch, garage or house at night for about a week. This will acclimatize them to your garden.

Seedling on left is root bound.

Starting from Seed

than that may be unreasonable. This is why many gardeners start a few specialty plants themselves, but purchase the bulk of their annuals already started from a garden center.

Each plant in this book will have specific information on starting it from seed, but there are a few basic steps that can be followed for all seeds. Cell-packs in trays with plastic dome covers are the easiest way for the home gardener to start seeds. They keep roots separated, and the tray and dome keep moisture in.

Seeds can also be started in pots, peat pots or peat pellets. The advantage to starting in peat pots or pellets is that you will not disturb the roots when you transplant your annuals. When planting out peat pots be sure to remove the top couple of inches of pot. If any of the pot is sticking up out of the soil it can wick moisture away from your plant.

Use a growing mix (soil mix) that is intended for seedlings. These mixes are very fine; usually made from peat moss, vermiculite and perlite. The mix will have good water holding capacity and will have been sterilized in order to prevent pests and diseases from attacking your tender young seedlings. It is heartbreaking to watch the tiny plants you have watched sprout from seeds flop over and die from damping off. Damping off is caused by a variety of soilborne fungi. The seedling will appear to have been pinched at soil level resulting in the

*S*tarting annuals from seed can be fun and will provide you with a wider variety of annuals than those available at a garden center. There are dozens of catalogs from different growers offering a varied selection of annuals that you can start from seed. Many gardeners while away chilly winter evenings by pouring through seed catalogs and planning their spring and summer gardens.

Starting your own annuals can save you money, particularly if you have a large area to plant. The basic equipment necessary is not expensive and most seeds can be started in a sunny window. You may, however, encounter a problem of limited space. One or two trays of annuals don't take up too much room, but storing more seedling toppling over. The pinched area blackens and the seedling dies. This problem is avoided through the use of sterile soil mix, evenly moist soil and good air circulation.

Fill your pots or seed trays with the soil mix and firm it down slightly. Soil that is too firmly packed will not drain well. Wet the soil before planting your seeds to prevent them from getting washed around. Large seeds can be planted one or two to a cell, but smaller seeds may have to be placed into a folded piece of paper and sprinkled evenly over the soil surface. Very tiny seeds, like those of begonia, can be mixed with fine sand before being sprinkled evenly across the soil surface. Mixing with sand will evenly space the seeds.

Tiny and small seeds will not need to be covered with any more soil, but medium size seeds can be lightly covered and large seeds can be poked into the soil. Some seeds need to be exposed to light in order to germinate and these should be left on the soil surface regardless of their size.

Place pots or flats of seeds in plastic bags to retain humidity while the seeds are germinating. Many planting trays come with clear plastic covers which can be placed over the trays to keep the moisture in. Remove the plastic once the seeds have germinated.

Water seeds and small seedlings with a fine spray from a hand-held mister—small seeds can easily be washed around if the spray is too strong.

Potting up seedlings

I recall working at a greenhouse where the sweet alyssum seed trays were once watered a little too vigorously. Sweet alyssum was soon found growing just about everywhere—with other plants, in the gravel on the floor, even in some of the flowerbeds. The lesson is 'water gently.' A less hardy species would not have come up at all if its seeds were washed into an adverse location.

Small seedlings will not need to be fertilized until they have about four or five true leaves. Seeds provide all the energy and nutrients that young seedlings require. Fertilizer will cause the plants to have soft growth that is more susceptible to insects and diseases and too strong a fertilizer can burn tender young roots. When the first leaves that sprouted begin to shrivel the plant has used up all its seed energy and you can begin to use a fertilizer diluted to a quarter strength when feeding seedlings or young plants.

If the seedlings get too big for their containers before you are ready to plant them out you may have to pot them up to avoid them becoming root-bound. Harden plants off by gradually exposing them to the sunnier, windier and fluctuating outdoor temperatures for increasing periods of time every day for at least a week.

Some seeds can be started directly in the garden. The procedure is similar to that of starting seeds indoors. Start with a well-prepared bed that has been smoothly raked. The small furrows left by the rake with help hold moisture and prevent the seeds from being washed away. Sprinkle the seeds onto the soil and cover them lightly with peat moss or more

California Poppy

Baby's Breath, Poppy and Mallow

soil. Larger seeds can be planted slightly deeper into the soil. You may not want to sow very tiny seeds directly in the garden because they can blow or wash away. The soil should be kept moist to ensure even germination. Use a gentle spray to avoid washing the seeds into undesirable locations in the bed. Covering your newly seeded bed with chicken wire, on old sheet or some thorny branches will discourage pets from digging.

Some seeds are easier than others to sow directly in the garden. Annuals with large seeds, quick germinating seeds or the seeds of annuals that are difficult to transplant are good choices for direct sowing.

ANNUALS FOR DIRECT-SEEDING

Amaranth
Baby's Breath
Bachelor's Button
Black-eyed Susan
Calendula
California Poppy
Candytuft
Chrysanthemum
Cockscomb
Cosmos
Forget-me-not
Godetia
Mallow
Nasturtium
Phlox
Poppy
Rocket Larkspur
Spider Flower
Sunflower
Sweet Pea
Zinnia

Planting Annuals

Once your annuals are hardened off it is time to plant them out. If your beds are already prepared you are ready to start. The only tool you are likely to need is a trowel. Be sure you have set aside enough time to do the job. You don't want to have young plants out of their pots and not finish planting them. If they are left out in the sun they can quickly dry out and die. To help avoid this problem choose an overcast day for planting out.

Moisten the soil to ease the removal of the plants from their containers. The plants may come out by pushing on the bottom of the cell or pot with your thumb. If the plants were growing in an undivided tray then you will have to gently untangle the roots. Very tangled roots can be separated by immersing them in water and washing some of the soil away. This should free the plants from one another. If you must handle the plant, hold it by a leaf to avoid crushing the stems. Remove and discard any damaged leaves or growth.

The root-ball should contain a network of white plant roots. If the root-ball is densely matted and twisted, break it apart in order to encourage the roots to extend and grow outward. Do so by breaking apart the tangles a bit with your thumbs. New root growth will start from the breaks allowing the plant to spread outwards.

Informal planting

bedding-out patterns are still used in many parks and formal gardens. Today's plantings can be made in casual groups and natural drifts. The quickest way to space out your annuals is to remove them from their containers and casually place them onto the bed. This will allow you to mix colors and plants without too much planning. Plant a small section at a time—don't allow the plants to dry out, especially if you have a large bed to plant.

If you are just adding a few annuals here and there to accent your shrub and perennial plantings then plant in groups. Random clusters of three to five plants adds color and interest to the constantly changing environment of your garden.

Insert your trowel into the soil and pull it towards you creating a wedge. Place your annual into the hole and firm the soil around the plant with your hands. Water newly planted annuals gently but thoroughly. They will need regular watering for a couple of weeks until they become established.

You don't have to be conservative when arranging your flowerbeds. There are more design choices than simple straight rows, though formal

Formal planting

Combine the low-growing or spreading annuals with tall or bushy ones. Keep the tallest plants towards the back and smallest plants towards the front of the bed. This improves the visibility of the plants and hides the often unattractive lower limbs of taller plants. Be sure also to leave your plants enough room to spread. They may look lonely and far apart when you first plant them, but annuals will quickly grow to fill in the space you leave.

There are no strict rules when it comes to planting and spacing. If you like your annuals in straight rows or in a jumble of colors, shapes and sizes then by all means plant them this way. The idea is to have fun and to create something that you will enjoy once your garden is planted.

Care of Annuals

*S*ome annuals require more care than others do, but most require minimal care once established. Ongoing maintenance will keep your garden looking its best. Weeding, watering, pinching, dead-heading and fertilizing are the basic tasks that when performed regularly can save you a big job later on.

Weeding

Keeping weed populations low keeps the garden healthy, neat and well tended. Weeding may not be your favorite task, but it is an essential one. Weeds compete with your plants for light, nutrients and space, and they can also harbor pests and diseases.

Weeds can be pulled by hand or with a hoe. Shortly after a rainfall, when the soil is soft and damp, is the easiest time to pull weeds. A hoe scuffed quickly across the soil surface will uproot small weeds and sever larger ones from their roots. Try to pull weeds out while they are still small. Once they are large enough to flower many will quickly set seed, then you will have an entire new generation to worry about.

Mulching

A layer of mulch around your plants will prevent weeds from germinating by preventing sufficient light from reaching the seeds. Those that do germinate will be smothered or will find it difficult to get to the soil surface, exhausting their energy before getting a chance to grow.

Mulch also helps maintain consistent soil temperatures and ensures that moisture is retained more effectively. In areas that receive heavy wind or rainfall, mulch can protect soil and prevent erosion. Mulching is effective in garden beds and planters.

Organic mulches include materials such as compost, bark chips, grass clippings or shredded leaves. These mulches add nutrients to soil as they break down, thus improving the quality of the soil and ultimately the health of your plants.

Mulched garden

Spread a couple of inches of mulch over the soil after you have planted your annuals. Don't pile the mulch too thick in the area immediately around the crowns and stems of your annuals. Mulch up against plants traps moisture, prevents air circulation and encourages fungal disease. As your mulch breaks down over summer be sure to replenish it with a thin layer of grass clippings, bark or compost.

Watering
Water thoroughly but infrequently. Annuals given a light sprinkle of water every day will develop roots that stay close to the soil surface making them vulnerable to heat and dry spells. Annuals given a deep watering once a week will develop a deeper root system. In a dry spell they will be adapted to seeking out the water trapped deeper in the ground. Use mulch to prevent water from evaporating out of the soil.

Be sure the water penetrates several inches into the soil. To save time, money and water you may wish to install an irrigation system. This can be as simple as laying soaker hoses around your garden beds under the mulch. Irrigation systems can be very complex or very simple depending on your needs; consult with your local garden center or landscape professionals for more information. When used properly, irrigation sytems can save you money by conserving water.

Annuals in hanging baskets and planters will probably need to be watered more frequently than plants growing in the ground. The smaller the container the more often the plants will need watering. Most containers and hanging moss baskets will need to be watered twice daily during sunny weather.

Fertilizing
Your local garden center should carry a good supply of both organic and chemical fertilizers. Follow the directions carefully because using excessive fertilizer can kill your plants by burning their roots. Whenever possible, use organic fertilizers because they are generally in lower concentrations and less likely to burn your plants.

Many annuals will flower most profusely if they are fertilized regularly. Some gardeners fertilize hanging baskets and container gardens every time they water—use a very dilute fertilizer so as not to burn the plants. However, too much fertilizer can result in plants that produce weak growth that is susceptible to pest and disease problems. Some plants, like nasturtiams, grow better without fertilizer and may produce few or no flowers when fertilized excessively.

Fertilizer comes in many forms. Liquids or water-soluble powders are easiest to use when watering. Slow release pellets or granules are mixed into the garden or potting soil or sprinkled around the plant and left to work over summer.

Grooming

Good grooming will make your annuals look neater and flower more profusely. Pinch out straggly growth and the tips of leggy annuals and remove the spent flowers of others to keep your garden neat and reduce pests and diseases.

Plants growing in cell-packs may have developed tall and straggly growth in an attempt to get light. Pinch back the long growth when planting out to encourage bushier growth.

Deadheading faded flowers keeps annuals looking healthy and attractive, promotes and prolongs continuous blooming and helps to prevent pest and disease problems. Get into the habit of picking off spent flowers as you are looking around your garden to save yourself a big job later. Some plants, such as impatiens and wax begonias, are self-cleaning, meaning that they drop their faded blossoms on their own.

If annuals appear to get tired and withered by midsummer, try trimming them back to encourage a second blooming. Mounding or low-growing annuals, like petunias, respond well to trimming. Take your garden shears and trim back a quarter or half the plant growth. New growth will sprout along with a new flush of flowers.

Some annuals have very tall growth and cannot be pinched. Instead, remove the main shoot after it blooms and side shoots may develop. Tall annuals, like candle larkspur, require staking with bamboo or other tall, thin stakes. Tie the plant loosely to the stake—strips of nylon hosiery make soft ties that won't cut into the plant. Stake bushy plants with twiggy branches or tomato cages. Insert the twigs or cages around the plant when it is small and it will grow to fill in and hide the stakes.

Impatiens

Annuals from Perennials

and treated as houseplants in the colder months. A process similar to hardening off is used to acclimatize plants to an indoor environment. Plants such as geraniums, black-eyed Susan vine and heliotrope, which are grown in the sun all summer, are gradually moved to shady garden spots. This gives them a chance to develop more efficient leaves, capable of surviving in limited light.

Perennials with tuberous roots can be stored over winter and replanted in late winter or early spring. Plants such as dahlias, tuberous begonias and four o'clock flower can be dug up in fall after the plant dies back but before the ground freezes. Shake the loose dirt away from the roots and let them dry out a bit in a cool dark place. Once they are dry, the rest of the soil should brush away. Dust the tubers with an anti-fungal powder (found at garden centers) before storing them in moist peat moss or coarse sawdust. Keep them in a cool, dark, dry place that doesn't freeze. Pot them if they start to sprout and keep them in a bright window and in moist soil. By late winter or early spring they should be potted so they will be ready for spring planting.

*M*any of the plants grown as annuals are actually perennials, e.g., geraniums, that originate in warmer climates and are unable to survive the colder winters, or biennials, e.g., forget-me-nots, which are started very early in the year to allow them to grow and flower in a single season. These perennials and biennials are listed as such in the species accounts. There are several techniques you can use in order to keep these plants for more than one summer.

Tropical perennials are given special treatment to help them survive winter, or they are simply brought inside

Cuttings can be taken from large, or fast-growing plants such as licorice plant and black-eyed Susan. Grow late-summer cuttings over winter for new spring plants. If winter storage sounds like too much work, replace them each year and leave the hard work to the growers.

Problems and Pests

*N*ew annuals are planted each spring and often different species are grown each year. These factors make it difficult for pests, which often have only a few preferred host plants, to establish a permanent population. However, because annual species are often grown together in masses, any problems that set in over summer are likely to attack all the plants.

For many years pest control involved spraying or dusting in an attempt to eliminate every garden pest. Experts now suggest a more moderate approach that aims to keep problems and the resulting damage at what is considered an acceptable level. As long as your annuals are still flowering and don't appear too chewed up or diseased, the damage should be considered acceptable. Chemicals, which can cause more harm than good, should only be used as a last resort. They tend to harm beneficial organisms as well as detrimental ones, leaving the garden vulnerable to inevitably greater problems. Chemical-free pest control is safer for the gardener, family members, pets and wildlife.

There are four steps involved in managing pests organically. Most important are the cultural controls. Next in importance are physical controls, followed by biological controls. Chemical controls should be used only when the first three options have proven unsuccessful.

Cultural controls involve the everyday gardening techniques used to care for your plants. Choosing varieties of annuals that are resistant to pests and disease, ensuring that each plant receives sufficient air circulation and preventing competition between plants for light, nutrients and space are cultural controls. If pests plague a certain type of plant each year, you may want to avoid that species in the future. Keeping garden tools clean and tidying up dead plant matter and fallen leaves at the end of the season are good practices.

Physical controls, typically used to deal with insect problems, include such tactics as picking insects off the plants by hand. This solution is very effective and not too time consuming

Bullfrogs eat many insect pests.

if you are able to catch the problem at an early stage. Large, slow insects in particular are easy to pick off. Other physical controls include barriers that prevent insects from reaching the plant and traps that catch or confuse the insect. The only effective physical control against diseases spreading may be to remove the infected part or possibly the entire plant.

Biological controls are natural predators. Birds, snakes, frogs, lady beetles, spiders and certain bacteria are just a few of the natural predators that can manage pest problems in your garden. Encourage their presence by installing a birdfeeder or birdbath. Birds will feast on many of the insects that attack your plants. Likely, there are many beneficial insects already residing in your yard. Avoid the use of chemical pesticides and provide food sources such as nectar—many annuals are nectar producers—to welcome predatory insects to your garden.

Chemical controls are a last resort. Remember that using chemicals also kills the beneficial insects in your garden. If you find chemical controls necessary, you should first consider organic options. Organic pesticides, while still poisonous, gradually break down into harmless components. Organic chemicals can be purchased at garden centers. Be sure to follow the directions carefully to avoid improper application that could harm your garden, your family or you.

Pests

APHIDS

Cluster along stems and on buds and leaves. Tiny; pear-shaped; winged or wingless; green, black, brown, red or gray. Suck sap from plants; cause distorted or stunted growth; sticky honeydew forms on the surfaces and encourages sooty-mold growth.

Squish small colonies by hand; brisk water spray dislodges them; many predatory insects and birds feed on them; spray serious infestations with insecticidal soap.

BEETLES

Some are beneficial, e.g., lady beetles; others, e.g., June beetles eat plants. Larvae: see borers and grubs. Many types and sizes; usually rounded in shape with hard shell-like outer wings covering membranous inner wings. Leave wide range of chewing damage; cause small or large holes in or around margins of leaves; entire leaf or areas between leaf veins are consumed; may also chew holes in flowers.

Pick beetles off at night and drop them into an old coffee can half filled with soapy water (soap prevents them from floating); spread an old sheet under plants and shake off beetles to collect and dispose of them.

BORERS

Larvae of some moths and beetles burrow into plant stems, leaves and/or roots. Worm-like; vary in size and get bigger as they bore through plants. Burrow and weaken stems to cause breakage; leaves will wilt; may see tunnels in leaves, stems or roots; rhizomes may be hollowed out entirely or in part.

Remove and destroy parts that are being bored; may be able to squish borers within leaves; may need to dig up and destroy infected roots and rhizomes.

BUGS (TRUE BUGS)

Many are beneficial; a few are pests. Small, up to ½" (1 cm) long; green, brown, black or brightly colored and patterned. Pierce plants to suck out sap; toxins may be injected that deform plants; sunken areas are left where pierced; leaves rip as they grow; leaves, buds and new growth may be dwarfed and deformed.

Remove debris and weeds from around plants in fall to destroy over-wintering sites; pick off by hand and drop into soapy water; spray with insecticidal soap.

CUTWORMS

Larvae of some moths. About 1" (2.5 cm) long; plump, smooth-skinned caterpillars; curl up when poked or disturbed. Usually only affects young plants and seedlings, which may have been completely consumed or chewed off at ground level.

Create barriers from old toilet tissue rolls to make collars around plant bases; push tubes at least halfway into ground.

Larvae of some moths are problematic.

within leaves leaving winding trails; tunneled areas lighter in color than rest of leaf; unsightly rather than health risk to plants.

Remove and destroy infected foliage; remove debris from area in fall to destroy overwintering sites; attract parasitic wasps with nectar plants.

Slugs & Snails
Common pest in Northwestern gardens. Slugs lack shells; snails have a spiral shell; slimy, smooth skin; can be up to 8" (20 cm) long, many are smaller; gray, green , black, beige, yellow or spotted. Leave large ragged hole in leaves and silvery slime trails on and around plants.

Grubs
Larvae of different beetles; problematic in lawns; may feed on plant roots. Commonly found below soil level; usually curled in a C–shape; body is white or gray; head may be white, gray, brown or reddish. Eat roots; plant is wilting despite regular watering; entire plant may pull out of the ground with only a gentle tug in severe cases.

Toss any grubs you find while digging onto a stone path or patio for birds to find and devour; control populations by applying parasitic nematodes or milky disease spore to infested soil (ask at your local garden center).

Leafminers
Larvae of some flies. Tiny; stubby maggots; yellow or green. Tunnel

Attach strips of copper to wood around raised beds or smaller boards inserted around susceptible groups of plants; slugs and snails will get shocked if they try to cross copper surfaces; pick them off by hand in the evening; spread wood ash or diatomaceous earth (available in garden centers) on ground around plants, which will pierce their soft bodies and cause them to dehydrate.

Spider Mites
Almost invisible to the naked eye; relatives of spiders without their insect-eating habits. Tiny; eight-legged; may spin webs; red, yellow or green; usually found on undersides of plant leaves. Suck juice out of leaves; may see fine webbing on leaves and stems; may see mites moving on leaf undersides; leaves

become discolored and speckled in appearance, then turn brown and shrivel up.

Wash spidermites off with a strong spray of water daily until all signs of infestation are gone; predatory mites are available through garden centers for ornamental plants or spray plants with insecticidal soap.

THRIPS
Difficult to see; may be visible if you disturb them by blowing gently on an infested flower. Tiny; slender; narrow fringed wings; yellow, black or brown. Suck juice out of plant cells, particularly flowers and buds, causing mottled petals and leaves, dying buds and distorted and stunted growth.

Remove and destroy infected plant parts; encourage native predatory insects with nectar plants; spray severe infestations with insecticidal soap.

RECIPE
INSECTICIDAL SOAP

You can make your own insecticidal soap at home.

Mix 1 tsp. (5 ml) of mild dish detergent or pure soap (biodegradable options are available) with 1 qt. (1 L) of water in a clean spray bottle.

Spray the surface areas of your plants and rinse them well within an hour of spraying.

WHITEFLIES
Tiny flying insects that flutter up into the air when the plant is disturbed. Tiny; moth-like; white; live on undersides of plant leaves. Suck juice out of plant leaves, causing yellowed leaves and weakened plants; leave sticky honeydew on leaves encouraging sooty mold growth.

Destroy weeds where insects may live; attract native predatory beetles and parasitic wasps with nectar plants ; spray severe cases with insecticidal soap.

Diseases

ANTHRACNOSE
Fungus. Yellow or brown spots on leaves; sunken lesions and blisters on stems; can kill plant.

Choose resistant varieties and cultivars; remove and destroy infected plant parts; thin out stems to improve air circulation; avoid handling wet foliage; keep soil well drained; clean up and destroy material from infected plants at end of growing season.

ASTER YELLOWS
Transmitted by insects called leafhoppers. Stunted or deformed growth; leaves yellowed and deformed; flowers dwarfed and greenish; can kill plant.

Control insects with insecticidal soap; remove and destroy infected plants; destroy any local weeds sharing these symptoms.

Botrytis Blight

Fungal disease. Leaves, stems and flowers blacken, rot and die.

Remove and destroy any infected plant parts; thin stems to improve air circulation, keep mulch away from base of plant, particularly in spring, when plant starts to sprout; remove debris from garden at end of growing season; do not over-water.

Leaf Spot

Two common types: one caused by bacteria and the other by fungus.

Bacterial: small speckled spots grow to encompass entire leaves; brown or purple in color; leaves may drop.

Fungal: black, brown or yellow spots causing leaves to wither.

Controls are similar for both types of leaf spot though bacterial infection is more severe. Remove and destroy infected plant parts; remove entire plant with bacterial infection and sterilize tools; avoid wetting foliage or touching wet foliage; remove debris at end of growing season.

Mildew

Two types: both are caused by fungus, but they have slightly different symptoms.

Downy mildew: yellow spots on upper sides of leaves and downy fuzz on the undersides; fuzz may be yellow, white or gray.

Powdery mildew: white or gray powdery coating on leaf surfaces that doesn't brush off (photo on p. 34).

Choose resistant cultivars; space plants well; thin stems to encourage air circulation; avoid wetting foliage or touching wet foliage; remove and destroy infected leaves or other parts; tidy any debris in fall.

Nematodes

Tiny worm-like organisms that give plants disease symptoms. One type infects foliage and stems the other infects roots.

Foliar: yellow spots that turn brown on leaves; leaves shrivel and wither; problem starts on lowest leaves and upwards.

Root knot: plant is stunted; may wilt; yellow spots on leaves; roots have tiny bumps or knots.

Remove infected plants; mulch soil; clean up debris in fall; don't touch wet foliage; add organic matter and parasitic nematodes to soil.

Rot

Several different fungi that affect different parts of the plant.

Crown rot: affects base of plant, causing stems to blacken and fall over and leaves to yellow and wilt; can kill plant.

Root rot: leaves yellow and plant wilts; digging up plant will show roots rotted away.

Keep soil well drained; don't damage plant if you are digging around it; keep mulches away from plant base; destroy infected plants.

RUST

Fungus. Pale spots on upper leaf surfaces; orange, fuzzy or dusty spots on leaf undersides.

Destroy infected plant parts; choose rust-resistant varieties and cultivars; avoid handling wet leaves; provide plant with good air circulation; clear up garden debris at end of season.

SOOTY MOLD

Fungus. Thin black film forms on leaf surfaces that reduces amount of light getting to leaf surfaces.

Wipe mold off leaf surfaces; control insects like aphids and whiteflies (honeydew left on leaves forms mold).

VIRUSES

Plant may be stunted and leaves and flowers distorted, streaked or dis-colored.

Viral diseases in plants cannot be controlled. Destroy infected plants; control insects like aphids, leaf-hoppers and whiteflies that spread disease.

WILT

If watering hasn't helped consider these two fungi.

Fusarium wilt: plant wilts, leaves turn yellow then die; symptoms generally appear first on one part of the plant before spreading to other parts.

Verticillium wilt: plant wilts; leaves curl up at edges; leaves turn yellow then drop off; plant may die.

Both wilts are difficult to control. Choose resistant varieties and cultivars; clean up debris at end of growing season; destroy infected plants; solarize soil before replanting (this may help if you've lost an entire bed of plants to these fungi).

Slug damaged plants

About This Guide

The annuals in this book are organized alphabetically by their common names. Additional common names and scientific names appear after the primary reference. We chose to use local common names instead of the sometimes less familiar scientific names. Later in each account, we describe recommended or alternate species, but keep in mind that many more hybrids, cultivars and varieties are often available. Check with your local greenhouses or garden centers when making your selection.

Quick identification information on flower color, height and spread are the first details given on each plant, followed by planting specifications. At the back of the book there is a Quick Reference Chart, p. 244, which is a handy guide to planning the species diversity in your garden.

Our region encompasses a broad geographical diversity, ranging from coastal sites to mountain tops. It is important to understand your relative proximity to the coast or mountain ranges and how far north or south you are in order to understand the duration, intensity and corresponding months of your seasons. The last frost date is specific to your area; refer to the map on p. 10 and consult your local garden centre. We have referred to the seasons in the general sense, because spring, for example, can occur any time between February and May, depending on where you garden.

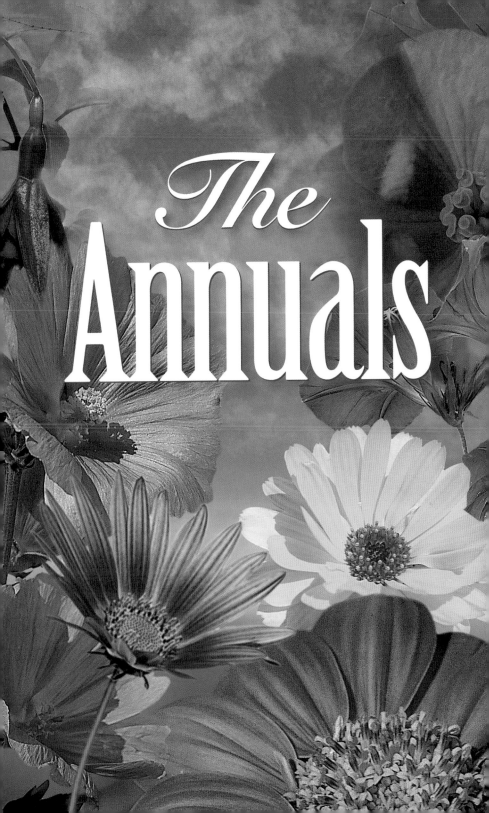

The
Annuals

African Daisy
Arctotis spp.

Flower color: Pink, orange, yellow, red or white.
Height: 12–24" (30–60 cm). **Spread:** 12–16" (30–40 cm).

*T*he best bed of African daisies I ever saw was alongside the south side of a modest beach house on the Oregon coast. This sunny spot was protected from rain by the overhang of the roof, but the daisy-like flowers could bask in the sun yet never feel the stress of afternoon temperatures over 80° F (27° C). African daisies are colorful and carefree plants when grown in sandy soil, full sun or cool coastal gardens. They make a lovely summer groundcover, perfect for a beach or vacation cabin.

PLANTING

Seeding: Indoors in early spring; direct sow after last frost.

Planting out: Once soil has warmed.

Spacing: 12–16" (30–40 cm).

GROWING

Choose a location in **full sun**. The soil should be **average, moist** and **well drained**. African daisies don't mind sandy soil, and they tolerate drought well, particularly if the weather isn't too hot.

Seeds started indoors should be planted in peat pots or peat pellets to avoid disturbing the roots when the seedlings are transplanted outdoors. Disturbed or damaged roots can cause the plants to take longer to become established. A plant may not recover at all if the damage is excessive. African daisy seeds do not keep, and new seed should be purchased or collected each year.

RECOMMENDED

There are several hybrids with striking flowers. They grow up to 20" (50 cm) tall and spread 12" (30 cm) wide. They do not come true from seeds and are propagated by cuttings.

A. stoechadifolia var. *grandis* has 3" (8 cm) wide blooms that are white with a yellow ring, and the undersides of the petals are pale lavender blue. The plant has a nice bushy form and grows 24" (60 cm) tall and 16" (40 cm) wide.

PROBLEMS & PESTS

These flowers do poorly in cold, wet weather. Watch for aphids, leafminers, downy mildew and leaf spots.

African daisies can be massed together in a sunny bed or border, and they do well in coastal gardens.

Deadheading prolongs the blooming season long into fall.

African daisies make interesting cut flowers, but they close up at night or if the room isn't bright enough.

Ageratum
Floss Flower
Ageratum houstonianum

Flower color: White, pink, mauve or blue.
Height: 6–24" (15–60 cm). **Spread:** About equal to height for shorter varieties; usually about half the height for taller varieties.

*S*ky blue ageratum combined with lemon yellow marigolds in a pot or bed was voted the most memorable display by one garden club's members. Think blue sky and summer sun to visualize the appeal of this blue-and-yellow color scheme. You can also pair the mauve and pink shades of puffy ageratum blooms with red salvia and lavender blue lobelia for a rich display of sunset colors.

Ageratum *is a genus with about 40 species of annuals, perennials and shrubs.*

PLANTING

Seeding: Indoors in early spring; direct sow after last frost.

Planting out: Once soil has warmed.

Spacing: about 4" (10 cm) for smaller varieties; about 12" (30 cm) for taller varieties.

GROWING

Ageratum prefers **full sun,** but it will tolerate partial shade. The soil should be **fertile, moist** and **well drained.**

Don't cover the seeds; they need light to germinate.

The smaller varieties, which become almost completely covered with the fluffy flowerheads, make excellent edging plants for flowerbeds as well as grouped in masses or grown in planters. The taller varieties are useful in the center of a flowerbed and make interesting cut flowers.

Naturalized in many warm areas, ageratum's diverse habitats range from tropical South America to warm-temperate North America.

The original species was a tall and leggy plant that was not considered attractive enough for the annual border but was often relegated to the cutting garden where the attractive flowers were cut for fresh arrangements. New cultivars are much more compact, and ageratum is now a proudly displayed annual.

RECOMMENDED

'Bavaria' grows about 10" (25 cm) tall with blue and white bicolored flowers.

Hawaii Series has compact, 6–8" (15–20-cm) tall plants with blue or white flowers.

'Swing Pink' is a compact, 6–8" (15–20-cm) tall plant with pink flowers.

GARDENING TIPS

These plants don't like to have their soil dry out, so they make good candidates for a moisture-retaining mulch, which will prevent you from having to water them too often. Don't mulch too thickly or too close to the base of the plant, or the plants may develop crown rot or root rot.

PROBLEMS & PESTS

Powdery mildew may become a problem. Be sure to plant ageratum in a location with good air circulation to help prevent powdery mildew and other fungal problems.

The genus name Ageratum *is derived from Greek and means 'without age,' a reference to the long-lasting flowers.*

Amaranth

Amaranthus spp.

Flower color: Red, yellow or green; flowers inconspicuous in some species.
Height: Usually 3–5' (90–150 cm); dwarf forms available.
Spread: 18–30" (45–75 cm).

*H*ot, bright colors give this plant a tropical look, and when the unusual, crimson, rope-like blooms drape over the foliage, this plant isn't just a color spot, it's a conversation piece! The old-fashioned name of the species 'love-lies-bleeding' will be easy to remember the first time you see the blood red flowers drip from the tops of the bushy plants. Use amaranth with other tropical-looking exotics, such as cannas and coleus, for a border that will shout with funky shapes and dance with chaotic color.

Several species of Amaranthus *are used as potherbs and vegetables because the leaves are high in protein; other species are grown as grain crops.*

PLANTING

Seeding: Indoors about three weeks before last frost; direct sow once soil has warmed.

Planting out: Once soil has warmed.

Spacing: 12–24" (30–60 cm).

GROWING

A location in **full sun** is preferable. The soil should be **poor to average** and **well drained**.

Seeds started indoors should be planted in peat pots or pellets to avoid disturbing the roots when transplanting them.

Don't give these plants rich soil or over-fertilize them, or their growth will be tall and soft and prone to falling over. Also, Joseph's coat will lose some of its leaf color when over-fertilized. The colors will be more brilliant in poorer soil.

A. caudatus

A. tricolor

RECOMMENDED

A. caudatus (love-lies-bleeding) has erect stems that support fluffy, long, red, yellow or green, drooping flowers that can be air dried. It grows to 36–60" (90–150 cm) tall and 18–30" (45–75 cm) wide.

A. tricolor (Joseph's coat) **'Illumination'** has hanging foliage in crimson and gold and inconspicuous flowers. It grows 4' (1.2 m) tall and 12" (30 cm) wide.

A. caudatus

GARDENING TIPS

Love-lies-bleeding is attractive grouped in borders, where it requires very little care or water over summer.

Love-lies-bleeding has the habit of self-seeding and showing up year after year. Unwanted plants are easy to uproot when they are young.

Joseph's coat is a bright and striking plant that is best used as an annual specimen plant rather than in a grouping, where it can quickly become overwhelming. It is also attractive when mixed with large foliage plants in the back of a border.

PROBLEMS & PESTS

Cold nights below 50° F (10° C) will cause leaf drop. Rust, leaf spot, root rot, aphids and some virus diseases are potential problems.

A. caudatus

A. tricolor

Baby's Breath

Gypsophila elegans

Flower color: White; some pink, red or mauve.
Height: Up to 24" (60 cm). **Spread:** 12–24" (30–60 cm).

*A*s white and pure as a newborn's christening gown, this delicate-looking flower with frothy, cloud-like blooms is a bit tricky to grow but worth the extra effort. In regions with little summer rainfall and more alkaline soil, baby's breath blooms with ease and softens the borders of any sunny flower garden. Use this flower to trim a display of heat-loving zinnias, glads or dahlias to create a living bouquet.

PLANTING

Seeding: Indoors in late winter; direct sow in mid-spring.

Planting out: Mid-spring.

Spacing: 8–18" (20–45 cm).

GROWING

Baby's breath grows best in **full sun**. The soil should be of **poor fertility,** and it should be **light, sandy** and **alkaline**. Allow the soil to dry out between waterings.

The clouds of flowers produced are ideal for rock gardens, rock walls, mixed containers or for mixing in borders with the bold-colored flowers of other plants. Baby's breath is native to the northeastern Mediterranean and looks very good when used in a Mediterranean-style garden.

Don't space the seedlings too far apart. The plants will flower more profusely if slightly crowded.

RECOMMENDED

'Covent Garden' has very large, white flowers and grows to 20" (50 cm) tall and 12" (30 cm) wide.

'Kermensia' has rose-colored flowers on 30" (75 cm) tall plants.

GARDENING TIPS

Add lime to the soil before planting. In fall or spring, before you plant, mix 1 cup (275 ml) of dolomitic lime into the planting hole.

Individual plants are short lived, so sow seeds successively for summer-long blooms.

PROBLEMS & PESTS

Most of the more common problems can be avoided by not over-watering the plants.

When seedlings first sprout, they need to be protected from slugs.

Baby's breath makes a wonderful addition to flower bouquets. The sprays of flowers can also be dried and used in fresh or dried arrangements.

Bachelor's Buttons
Cornflower
Centaurea cyanus

Flower color: Blue; some red, pink, white or occasionally violet.
Height: 8–32" (20–80 cm). **Spread:** 6–24" (15–60 cm).

*I*n a garden with poor, rocky or sandy soil, you can pair this tough and hard-to-kill annual with California poppies for a bright blue-and-gold color combo that will mimic the blue skies and summer sun. The Latin name means 'century,' and it refers to the folklore that this plant can live for a hundred years—it reseeds easily and outgrows most pest problems. The long life of the cut flowers makes them perfect for pinning to a lapel or poking through a button hole.

PLANTING

Seeding: Direct sow in early fall for spring blooms; in spring for summer bloom.

Planting out: Around last frost.

Spacing: According to expected spread of variety, generally 12–24" (30–60 cm).

Bachelor's buttons is useful in a mixed border and for cut flowers, and it is popular for cottage and other informal gardens.

GROWING

Bachelor's buttons will do best in **full sun**.
Fertile, moist, well-drained soil is preferable,
but any soil, including poor and dry soil, is
tolerated. Light frost won't harm the plants.

Seed started indoors in March should be planted
in peat pots or pellets to avoid disturbing the
roots when transplanting them.

RECOMMENDED

'Blue Boy' has rich blue flowers. It grows to 39"
(100 cm) tall and spreads up to 30" (75 cm) wide.

Polka Dot Mixed is a bushy, dwarf plant growing
18" (45 cm) tall. It flowers in a variety of colors.

GARDENING TIPS

Shear back spent flowers and old foliage in
midsummer for fresh new growth.

PROBLEMS & PESTS

Aphids, downy mildew and powdery mildew
may cause problems.

Bacopa

Sutera cordata

Flower color: White or pinkish purple.
Height: 3–5" (8–13 cm). **Spread:** 12–20" (30–50 cm).

*T*his low-growing, draping plant continues to bloom and bloom. Among the first plants to show color in cool spring weather when draped with small, star-like blooms, bacopa continues to be covered with fresh white or subtle lavender blossoms through the heat of summer and the cooler weather of fall. It is perfect for spilling from window boxes and container gardens or as a groundcover along the edge of a pathway. I discovered bacopa several years ago as a new introduction and now consider it my best choice for filling the garden with carefree color.

PLANTING

Seeding: Not recommended.

Planting out: Once soil has warmed up.

Spacing: 12" (30 cm).

GROWING

Bacopa grows equally well in **full sun or partial shade**. The soil should be of **average fertility, humus rich, moist** and **well drained**. Don't allow this plant to completely dry out; the leaves will die quickly if they become dry.

Bacopa is a popular plant for hanging baskets, mixed containers and window boxes. It will form an attractive spreading mound in a rock garden, but it will need to be watered regularly.

RECOMMENDED

'Olympic Gold' has green and gold variegated foliage with white flowers.

'Snowflake' has densely held, heart-shaped leaves, with scalloped edges. Tiny, star-shaped, white flowers cover the neat trailing stems. **'Giant Snowflake'** is a more vigourous development of 'Snowflake.'

GARDENING TIPS

Cutting back the dead growth may encourage new shoots to form.

PROBLEMS & PESTS

Whitefly and other small insects can become a real menace on this plant, because the tiny leaves and dense growth create the perfect hiding spots for small insects.

'Olympic Gold'

Bacopa is a perennial that is grown as an annual outdoors. It will thrive as a houseplant in a bright room.

'Giant Snowflake'

'Snowflake'

Begonia

Begonia spp.

Flower color: Pink, white, red, yellow, orange, bicolored or picotee.
Height: Varies from 6–24" (15–60 cm). **Spread:** Varies from 6–24" (15–60 cm).

*T*here are many begonias: some are grown as houseplants, others make excellent additions to annual gardens. Begonias are perennials that are commonly grown as annuals. Wax begonias, so called because of their thick, shiny leaves, are generally small and mound-forming. They are sometimes called 'fibrous begonias' to describe their root system. The tuberous begonias have larger blooms and tuberous roots. Tuberous begonias are available in upright and pendulous forms.

PLANTING

Seeding: Indoors in early winter.

Planting out: Once soil has warmed.

Spacing: According to spread of variety.

GROWING

Light or partial shade is best, although some

B. × tuberhybrida

of the new varieties of wax begonia are sun tolerant. The soil should be **fertile, rich in organic matter** and **well drained** with a **neutral or acidic pH.** Allow the soil to dry out between waterings.

Begonias can be tricky to grow from seed. The seeds are tiny and require warm temperatures and light to germinate (do not cover). Keep the soil surface moist but not soggy and maintain daytime temperature at 70–80° F (21–27° C) and above 50° F (10° C) at night. Begonias can be potted up individually once they are large enough (with three or four leaves) to handle. Tubers can also be purchased in early spring and started indoors.

Begonias are also grown for their attractive and colorful foliage. Use the dark-leaved forms of wax begonias for splashes of contrasting color next to silver lamiums and gray-leaved licorice plants.

B. semperflorens

B. semperflorens

Wax begonias are the ideal flower for lazy gardeners because they will continue to bloom all summer, even without deadheading.

B. × tuberhybrida

All begonias are useful plants for planting in shaded garden beds and planters. The hanging tuberous varieties can also be used in hanging baskets and along rock walls where they can be seen drooping over the edges. Wax begonias have a neat rounded habit that makes them particularly attractive as a edging plant. They can also be paired with roses and geraniums in a frontyard bed for a formal look.

RECOMMENDED

B. semperflorens (wax begonias) have pink, white, red or bicolored flowers and green, bronze, reddish or variegated with white foliage. The plants are 6–14" (15–35 cm) tall and 6–24" (15–60 cm) wide. **'Pizzazz'** has plants with green leaves that hold up in bad weather. **Cocktail Series** is a dwarf plant, 6–12" (15–30 cm) tall and 12" (30 cm) wide, with bronze foliage. Flowers are red, pink, white or bicolored.

B. x *tuberhybrida* (tuberous begonias) are a group of varieties sold as tubers. They come in many shades of red, pink, yellow, orange, white and picotee (margins are colored differently from main petal color), and the plants are 8–24" (20–60 cm) tall and wide. **Non-stop Series** can be started from seed and grows about 12" (30 cm) tall with an equal spread; double and semi-double flowers come in pink, yellow, orange, red and white.

GARDENING TIPS

Choose the bronze leaf varieties of wax begonias over the ones with green leaves if you are planting in a sunny location.

Wax begonias can be dug out of the garden before the first frost and grown as houseplants in winter in a bright room.

The tubers of tuberous begonias can be uprooted at the end of the season, when the foliage dies back, and stored in slightly moistened peat moss over winter. The tuber will sprout new shoots in late winter and can be potted up for another season of flowering.

PROBLEMS & PESTS

The plant may get root or leaf rot if over-watered. A few other problems may occur, such as whiteflies and spider mites, but they are infrequent.

B. semperflorens

Bells-of-Ireland

Moluccella laevis

Flower color: Green.
Height: 24–36" (60–90 cm). **Spread:** 9" (23 cm).

These sun-loving, tall and spiky flowers were not originally from Ireland but rather the eastern Mediterranean. Regardless of origin, the unusual green color of the blossoms makes them a favorite of florists in St. Patrick's Day arrangements. Pair this flower up with shasta daisies for a contrast in color and form, or use bright yellow coreopsis at the feet of these flowering spikes to achieve a cool lemon-lime color. You won't need the luck of the Irish to grow these annuals from seed—they pop out of the warm soil and grow tall at an impressive rate. I often recommend bells-of-Ireland to beginner gardeners who want a maximum return on their energy investment.

PLANTING

Seeding: Indoors in mid-winter; direct sow in mid-spring for summer flowers or in late summer for fall flowers.

Planting out: After last frost.

Spacing: 12" (30 cm).

GROWING

Bells-of-Ireland prefers to grow in **full sun** but will tolerate partial shade. The soil should be of **average or good fertility** and **well drained**. When seeding, don't cover the seeds because they need light to germinate.

Use these plants at the back of a border—the green spikes create an interesting backdrop for more brightly colored flowers.

These plants are popular in fresh or dried flower arrangements. When hung upside down to dry, the green cups become white or beige and take on a papery texture.

Black-Eyed Susan
Coneflower
Rudbeckia hirta

Flower color: Yellow, orange, red or sometimes bicolored;
with brown or green centers.
Height: 12–36" (30–90 cm). **Spread:** 12–18" (30–45 cm).

*T*he daisy form of this flower has a distinctive beauty with its lime green or brown eye surrounded by rich red, yellow or orange petals. It is especially attractive when grown against the side of a wooden barn or outhouse, or when allowed to bloom along a rustic split-rail fence. Pair this mounding country flower with vertical spikes of ornamental grass for a low-maintenance country display; or poke holes in the bottom of a rusting metal wash tub, add potting soil and let the warm color and friendly face of the gloriosa daisy turn trash into treasure.

PLANTING

Seeding: Indoors in late winter; direct sow in mid-spring.

Planting out: Late spring.

Spacing: 18" (45 cm).

GROWING

Black-eyed Susan grows equally well in **full sun or partial shade,** in a clay soil of **average or high fertility** with plenty of **moist organic matter**.

'Irish Eyes'

Black-eyed Susan can be planted individually or in groups. Use them in beds and borders, large containers, meadow plantings and wildflower gardens. They will bloom well even in the hottest part of the garden.

This tough flower will have long-lasting blooms to keep fall flowerbeds bright.

R. hirta

Gloriosa Daisy Mix

RECOMMENDED

Gloriosa Daisy Mixed has large flowers, up to 6"
(15 cm) across, in warm shades of gold and
brown. Plants grow up to 36" (90 cm) tall.

'Indian Summer' has huge flowers, 6–9"
(15–23 cm) across, on sturdy plants, which
grow 36" (90 cm) tall or taller.

'Irish Eyes' has single flowers, with a clear green
eye. Plants grow up to 30" (75 cm) tall.

'Toto' is a dwarf cultivar that grows 10–12"
(25–30 cm) tall. This cultivar is small enough to
include in planters.

GARDENING TIPS

Keep cutting the flowers to promote more blooming—black-eyed Susan makes a good vase flower.

If it is growing in loose, moist soil, black-eyed Susan will reseed itself.

R. hirta is a perennial that is grown as an annual. It is not worth trying to keep over winter because it grows and flowers quickly from seed.

PROBLEMS & PESTS

Slugs and snails can be a problem on young plants. Aphids and powdery mildew can also cause the occasional problem.

Black-eyed Susan is a brightly flowered native plant that makes an excellent addition to wildflower and natural gardens.

'Irish Eyes'

Black-Eyed Susan Vine
Thunbergia alata

Flower color: Yellow, orange or cream white, usually with dark centers.
Height: Over 5' (1.5 m).
Spread: Can be trained to spread as much as desired.

*T*he friendly golden face of black-eyed Susan twirling around a rustic twig arbor or climbing up a tee-pee of poles inserted into a half-barrel planter gives a cheerful country look. A wire or cyclone fence or even a rose plant with naked knees can also be a support system for this dark-eyed country gal. I've found this vine to be the perfect accent in the garden each summer. I remove the seat of a chair, replace the cushion with a chicken wire and moss lining, fill this hole with potting soil and plant black-eyed Susan vine, alyssum and bacopa. By late summer, the garden chair is overflowing with flowers, and the vine is twining up the back and over the sides of this unusual container.

PLANTING

Seeding: Indoors in mid-winter; direct sow in mid-spring.

Planting out: Late spring.

Spacing: 12–18" (30–45 cm).

GROWING

Black-eyed Susan vine grows well in **full sun, partial shade or light shade**. Grow in **fertile, moist** and **well drained** soil that is **high in organic matter**.

Black-eyed Susan vine can be trained to twine around fences and walls as well as up trees and over shrubs. It is also attractive trailing down from the top of a rock garden or wall or growing in mixed containers and hanging baskets. It can be brought into the house over winter then returned to the garden the following spring—it is a perennial treated as an annual.

RECOMMENDED

Susie Series has vines that grow 5' (1.5 m) long, and the large flowers can be yellow, orange or white.

ALTERNATE SPECIES

T. gregorii has orange flowers with no black eye. The plant can grow to 15' (5 m) long or longer.

GARDENING TIPS

These vines can be quite vigorous and may need to be trimmed back from time to time, particularly if the plant is brought inside for winter. To bring in for winter, acclimatize the plant to the lower light levels by gradually moving it to more shaded locations. Keep it in a bright room out of direct sunlight for winter. The following spring the plant can be hardened off before moving it outdoors.

Fashion wire frames into any desired shape to grow black-eyed Susan vine into whimsical topiary. An old rocking horse can be put out to pasture as a frame for this vine.

Blanket Flower
Gaillardia pulchella

Flower color: Red, orange or yellow, often in combination.
Height: 10–18" (25–45 cm) or taller. **Spread:** 12" (30 cm).

*I*f you've been disappointed with the blooming results or the care needed for sunny window boxes, try filling them with the small, but bright, blooms of blanket flower. This plant is heat-resistant and will drape over the sides of the box in gentle waves of color. Grow blanket flower with nasturtiums and other annuals that don't require fertile, moist soil, and you will have flowers covering all the hard-to-grow areas of your garden. Blanket flower can even bloom in a bed of rocks and sandy soil.

PLANTING

Seeding: Indoors in late winter; direct sow in mid-spring.

Planting out: Mid- to late spring.

Spacing: 12" (30 cm).

GROWING

Blanket flower prefers **full sun**. The soil should be of **poor or average fertility, light, sandy** and **well drained**.

The less water this plant receives, the better it will do. Once the weather begins to dry up for summer, plant blanket flower in a location where it will not get watered with other plants. Blanket flower is the plant to use in the area of the garden that you always forget to water.

Don't cover the seeds because they need light to germinate. They also require warm soil.

Blanket flower has an informal, sprawling habit that makes it a perfect addition to an informal cottage garden or mixed border. Being drought-tolerant, it is well suited to exposed, sunny slopes, where it can help retain soil while more permanent plants are growing in.

RECOMMENDED

Plume Series has double flowerheads in vibrant shades of red or yellow. It grows about 12" (30 cm) tall, with an equal spread, and has a uniform dwarf growth habit and long blooming time.

GARDENING TIPS

Deadhead to encourage more blooms.

PROBLEMS & PESTS

Many problems you are likely to encounter with this plant can be avoided by not over-watering. Aphids, slugs and snails may be troublesome.

Blue Lace Flower

Trachymene coerulea

Flower color: Pale lavender blue or white.
Height: 24" (60 cm). **Spread:** 9–12" (23–30 cm).

By adding these delicate sprays of lavender blue flowers to your garden, you will be putting out the welcome mat for butterflies and giving a soft, elegant quality to the display. These flowers look best when grouped with companions because the foliage is delicate and the stems are rather long and awkward. Pink or white wax begonias or the perennial *Heuchera* 'Palace Purple' make good bedfellows for this lovely flower.

PLANTING

Seeding: Indoors in late winter; direct sow once soil has warmed.

Planting out: After last frost.

Spacing: 12" (30 cm).

GROWING

Blue lace flower prefers a **sheltered location in full sun** that isn't too hot. It enjoys cool night temperatures. The soil should be of **average fertility, light** and **well drained**.

Direct sow the seeds into the garden because the seedlings dislike being transplanted. If you do start them indoors, sow the seeds in individual peat pots. The seeds can be slow to germinate.

Blue lace flower is used in beds and borders and is generally combined with other plants. The plants are quite erect, and with their delicate, feathery foliage they look good in an informal cottage style garden. The flowers are long lasting when used in fresh arrangements.

RECOMMENDED

'Lace Veil' is a fragrant white variety.

GARDENING TIPS

Insert forked branches around young plants to keep them from flopping over in rain and wind.

Blue Marguerite

Blue Daisy

Felicia amelloides

Flower color: Many shades of blue or white with yellow centers.
Height: 12–24" (30–60 cm). **Spread:** 12–24" (30–60 cm) or wider.

*I*f you garden along the cool coastline, you can enjoy blue Marguerites rivaling the ocean with their waves of color. This flower's carefree, casual form and blue petals makes it a good contrast with the more stiff and upright form of a pink impatiens or coral-colored begonia.

PLANTING

Seeding: Indoors in winter; direct sow in midsummer.

Planting out: After last frost.

Spacing: 12" (30 cm).

GROWING

Blue Marguerite likes to grow in **full sun**. The soil should be of **average fertility** and **well drained**. These plants do not tolerate heat well.

Blue Marguerite, with its sprawling habit, is well suited to rock gardens, bed edges, mixed containers and hanging baskets. The flowers will close at night and on cloudy days.

RECOMMENDED

'Astrid Thomas' is a dwarf variety with medium-blue flowers. It grows to 10" (25 cm) tall, with an equal spread.

'Midnight' has deep blue flowers.

GARDENING TIPS

The key to keeping these plants looking their best is trimming. When they are young, pinch the tips to promote bushiness. Deadhead while they are in flower and cut the plants back when the flowering slows down during summer. Once summer ends they will produce a second flush of growth and flowers.

Take cuttings from the new fall growth to start plants for the following spring. This will save you the uncertainty of starting with seeds or the trouble of trying to overwinter entire large plants.

PROBLEMS & PESTS

Blue Marguerites are generally trouble free, although aphids may be a problem.

Felicias are sometimes called kingfisher daisies. The bright blue color of the flowers is like the plumage of the European kingfisher.

Blue Marguerite will do well as a houseplant if it is grown in a sunny location.

Browallia
Amethyst Flower
Browallia speciosa

Flower color: Violet, blue or white.
Height: 10–20" (25–50 cm). **Spread:** 8–12" (20–30 cm).

*T*he bell-shaped blooms on these low-growing plants usually come in shades of blue and violet that will mix well in cottage garden plantings. The clear white variety provides contrast with other flowers, such as dianthus or lobelia, in the front of the border. The cup-shape of the blooms looks especially nice when placed in the foreground of taller plants with similar blooms, such as larkspur or hollyhock.

PLANTING

Seeding: Indoors in late winter.

Planting out: Once soil has warmed.

Spacing: 8–10" (20–25 cm).

GROWING

Browallia prefers **partial shade,** but it will tolerate full sun. The soil should be **fertile** and **well drained**.

Do not cover the seeds when you plant them, because they need light to germinate.

Grow browallia in mixed borders, mixed containers or hanging baskets. Pinch flowers often to encourage new growth and more blooms.

RECOMMENDED

Jingle Bells Series includes **'Blue Bells,' 'Marine Bells,' 'Silver Bells'** and **'White Bells.'** They vary in size from 8" (20 cm) to 12" (30 cm) in both height and spread.

Troll Series includes **'Blue Troll'** and **'White Troll,'** which are more compact and bushy in form, making them suitable for pots. They grow about 10" (25 cm) tall.

GARDENING TIPS

Browallias can be grown as houseplants year-round or brought indoors at the end of the season to be used as houseplants during winter. They do not like the cold, so wait several weeks after the last frost before setting out the plants.

PROBLEMS & PESTS

Browallias are generally problem free. Whiteflies may cause some trouble but can be controlled with insecticidal soap. The soap may discolor the flowers if it is not sprayed in the shade or if it is not rinsed off the plants with clean water about an hour after spraying. A gentle mist or spray from a garden hose gives a good rinse.

Butterfly Flower
Poor Man's Orchid
Schizanthus pinnatus

Flower color: Pink, red, yellow or purple; usually bicolored.
Height: 6–24" (15–60 cm). **Spread:** 9–12" (23–30 cm).

*T*he most spectacular hanging baskets I've ever admired can be seen each June hanging from the lightposts in the city center of Victoria, B.C. Butterfly flowers flow over the edges of these baskets and bloom happily in a cocktail of flower shapes and forms. Most of the blooms have two or more colors on the orchid-like petals, so these flowers mix well with many different plants. They are at their peak in early summer before high temperatures fade their glory. In flowerbeds, they grow well in a rich tapestry of blooms with other early summer bloomers, such as pansies and brachycomb.

PLANTING

Seeding: Indoors in mid-winter.

Planting out: After last frost.

Spacing: 12" (30 cm).

GROWING

Butterfly flower grows best in **full sun**. The soil should be **fertile, moist** and **well drained**.

The seeds should be planted on the soil surface. Keep the entire container in darkness or cover it with dark plastic or newspaper to promote even germination. Remove the cover once the seeds have sprouted.

Butterfly flower can be used in beds, borders, rock gardens and mixed containers. It does best in cool summer climates.

RECOMMENDED

Dwarf Bouquet Mixed has shorter, more compact plants—usually no taller than 16" (40 cm)—that are good in pots.

Royal Pierrot Mixed has rich colors and is good in hanging baskets.

'Star Parade' is a compact variety available in several colors. It grows up to 10" (25 cm) tall.

GARDENING TIPS

These plants have a short flowering season, but you can extend the bloom time with successive sowings. Alternately, you can replace them with late summer- and fall-blooming mums halfway through summer.

Butterfly flower can be grown as an indoor potted plant in a bright window.

'Star Parade'

Butterfly flowers are colorful and long lasting after they are cut; making them a good choice for fresh arrangements.

Calendula
Pot Marigold • English Marigold
Calendula officinalis

Flower color: Yellow, orange, cream, apricot or gold.
Height: 12–30" (30–75 cm). **Spread:** 12–18" (30–45 cm).

Calendula petals add a tangy heartiness to stews, soups and egg dishes, but they also make a garden look delectable. Use this edible flower to border a vegetable garden or to fill in a casual planter garden. Budget-wise gardeners will appreciate how quick and easy calendula is to grow from seed, filling large spaces with sturdy blooms that do especially well when summers are cool and cloudy. The daisy-like blooms repeat all summer if the plant is deadheaded. I broadly cast calendula seed in my rock garden and enjoy the surprise of seeing which crack or crevice will sprout golden blooms.

PLANTING

Seeding: Direct sow in mid-spring; indoors a month or so earlier.

Planting out: Mid-spring.

Spacing: 8–10" (20–25 cm).

GROWING

Calendula does equally well in **full sun or partial shade**. It likes cool weather and can withstand a light frost. The soil should be of **average fertility** and **well drained**.

Young plants are sometimes difficult to find in nurseries because they are quick and easy to grow from seed. A second sowing in early summer gives a good fall display.

These informal plants are attractive in borders and mixed into the vegetable patch. They can also be used in mixed planters.

RECOMMENDED

'Bon Bon Dwarf' is 10–12" (25–30 cm) tall and comes in all colors.

Kablouna Series has crested, double flowers in shades of yellow and orange. The plants grow 24" (60 cm) tall.

Princess Series has dark-centered flowers, which give the garden an old-fashioned country look.

PROBLEMS & PESTS

Calendulas are often trouble free, but they can have problems with aphids, whiteflies, slugs and snails, as well as smut, powdery mildew and fungal leaf spot. They usually continue to perform well even when they are afflicted with problems.

Calendula flowers are popular kitchen herbs that can be added to stews for color and flavoring or brewed into an infusion that can be used to wash minor cuts and bruises.

The flowers can be cut for arrangements.

California Poppy

Eschscholzia californica

Flower color: Orange, yellow or red; less commonly pink, violet or cream.
Height: 12–24" (30–60 cm). **Spread:** 6–12" (15–30 cm).

*I*f you have a gravel path or patch of dry infertile soil, California poppies will still bloom away contentedly. These cottage-garden reseeders pop up through cracks of a flagstone path or nearby rockery, cheerfully blooming anyplace the sun and well-drained soil meet. Pair California poppies with *Sedum* 'Autumn Joy' and blue bachelor buttons, which also tolerate these poor growing conditions.

PLANTING

Seeding: Early fall in mild climates; early spring in colder climates.

Spacing: 6–12" (15–30 cm).

GROWING

California poppies prefer **full sun** but will tolerate some shade. The soil should be of **poor or average fertility** and **well drained**. With too rich a soil, the plants will be lush and green but will bear few, if any, flowers. These plants are drought-tolerant once they are well established. Never start these plants indoors, because they dislike having their roots disturbed and they grow quickly in the garden.

Start seeds in early fall for blooms in spring or in early spring for blooms later in summer.

California poppies can be included in an annual border or annual planting in a cottage garden. You may notice that these plants self-seed wherever they are planted. This quality makes them perfect for naturalizing in a meadow garden or rock garden where they will come back from year to year.

RECOMMENDED

Ballerina Series has a mixture of colors and semi-double or double flowers.

GARDENING TIPS

The seeds are renowned for being difficult to germinate, because of the great quantity of water required for germination and for the development of the young plants. Until they are flowering, provide them with regular and frequent watering. Once they are flowering, they are more drought-tolerant.

PROBLEMS & PESTS

California poppies generally have few pest problems, but, occasionally fungi can trouble them.

Candytuft

Iberis spp.

Flower color: White, pink, purple or red.
Height: 6–18" (15–45 cm). **Spread:** 6–9" (15–23 cm).

*A*nnual candytuft looks softer and is more upright than the more common, trailing, perennial candytuft, which is grown as a rockery plant. The annual candytuft blooms in tints of pastel pink, rose and lavender to form puffs of color as soft as cotton candy. Grow candytuft in the dry, rocky soil at the base of a purple smoke tree, or contrast candytuft with the slender, upright forms of hot pink rose campion or lime green bells-of-Ireland.

PLANTING

Seeding: Indoors in late winter; outdoors around last frost.

Planting out: After last frost.

Spacing: 6" (15 cm).

GROWING

Candytuft prefers to grow in **full sun**. The soil should be of **poor or average fertility, well drained** and have a **neutral or alkaline pH**. These informal plants can be used in rock walls or mixed containers, or to edge beds.

Rocket candytuft is a good plant for blooming in late winter and early spring. For early bloom, start the seeds in the garden in fall.

RECOMMENDED

I. amara (rocket candytuft) has white flowers clustered densely on cone-shaped spikes. This species prefers the cooler climate of the Pacific Northwest. It grows up to 18" (45 cm) tall and spreads 6" (15 cm).

I. umbellata (globe candytuft) has flowers in shades of pink, purple, red or white. The plant grows 6–12" (15–30 cm) tall and spreads 9" (23 cm) or more.

PROBLEMS & PESTS

Keep an eye open for slugs and snails. Caterpillars can also be a problem. In poorly drained soil, several fungal problems may develop.

I. umbellata

If the plant seems to be blooming less often as summer progresses, trim it back lightly to promote new growth and more flowers.

I. umbellata

Canterbury Bells
Cup-and-Saucer Plant
Campanula medium

Flower color: Blue, lavender, purple, pink or white.
Height: 12–36" (30–90 cm), depending on variety. **Spread:** 6–12" (15–30 cm).

Fat, puffy blooms in true blue and shades of lavender make these flowers ring like country church bells. Grow the taller forms up against a picket fence, and use the lower varieties to spill from the top of a rock wall or to add summer color to a rock garden. These stately flowers are the pride of England, and they can put a bit of Britain in your own garden year after year because they will reseed themselves annually if you make them feel welcome.

PLANTING

Seeding: Indoors in mid-winter; direct sow in late summer in mild winter areas.

Planting out: Early spring.

Spacing: 6–12" (15–30 cm).

GROWING

Canterbury bells prefer **full sun** but will tolerate partial shade. The soil should be **fertile, moist** and **well drained**. These plants will not suffer if the weather cools or if there is a light frost. They transplant easily, even when in full bloom.

When seeding, leave seeds uncovered because they require light for germination. Protect fall-sown plants with mulch of small evergreen branches, and they will flower in late spring. For plants started indoors, harden off in a cold frame or on a sheltered porch before planting out.

These annuals are actually biennials.

When these informal plants are planted in small groups, they look good in a border or rock garden. The tallest varieties produce good flowers for cutting. Use dwarf varieties in planters.

RECOMMENDED

'Bells of Holland' is a dwarf cultivar. It has flowers in various colors and grows about 18" (45 cm) tall.

'Calycanthema' has double, bell-shaped flowers, one inside the other. The plant grows about 30" (75 cm) tall.

GARDENING TIPS

Canterbury bells make a good addition to a cottage garden or other informal garden where their habit of reseeding can keep them popping up year after year.

PROBLEMS & PESTS

Unfortunately, snails and slugs are fond of Canterbury bells.

Cape Marigold
African Daisy
Dimorphotheca sinuata

Flower color: White, orange, yellow or pink; often with brown, orange or purple centers. **Height:** 12–18" (30–45 cm). **Spread:** 12" (30 cm).

*I*t is the color combinations on this flower that makes it a daisy with a difference. The dark brown, orange or purple eyes are surrounded by thin petals that show off a second color on the undersides whenever the wind blows. These heat lovers like a hot, dry location in the blazing summer sun, and they'll stay as fresh looking as a daisy. Use rocks and gravel as companions in their bed, or pair them with a collection of sedums and succulents that also like the heat.

PLANTING

Seeding: Indoors in early spring; direct sow after last frost.

Planting out: After last frost.

Spacing: 12" (30 cm).

GROWING

Cape marigold likes to grow in **full sun**. The soil should be **light, fertile** and **well drained**. These plants are drought-resistant.

Cape marigolds are most attractive when planted in groups or masses. Use them in beds and borders. They can be cut for flower arrangements, although they close at night and on cloudy days. If your flower vase is in a dark spot in the house, the flowers might also close.

ALTERNATE SPECIES

D. pluvialis (cape marigold; rainy daisy) It is white with purple on the undersides of the petals and with purple at the base of the petals.

GARDENING TIPS

Cape marigolds do not grow well in wet coastal climates. Keep them from too much rain by planting under the eaves of the house in window boxes or raised beds.

PROBLEMS & PESTS

Problems are only likely to occur in hot and wet climates. Dry and cool places produce healthy plants that are less susceptible to disease. Planting these plants out as the seasonal rains begin to taper off will provide good growing conditions.

D. pluvialis

Take along your umbrella on days when the flowers of cape marigold remain closed. The blooms will not open if rain is forecast.

China Aster
Callistephus chinensis

Flower color: Purple, blue, pink, red, white, peach or yellow.
Height: 12–36" (30–90 cm). **Spread:** 10–18" (25–45 cm).

*T*he ruffled petals of China aster's remind me of a clown's collar and add a festive atmosphere to the garden. The colors are as loud and entertaining as a three-ring circus—these flowers steal the spotlight by performing all summer long. The various heights of this aster's cultivars mean that you can have a row of tall asters up against a fence or short types along a pathway. Pair these asters with other flowers, such as annual candytufts or delphiniums, that prefer an alkaline soil.

PLANTING

Seeding: Indoors in late winter;
direct sow after last frost.

Planting out: Once soil has warmed.

Spacing: 6–12" (15–30 cm).

GROWING

China asters prefer **full sun** but will tolerate partial shade. The soil should be **fertile, evenly moist**
and **well drained**. A pH that is neutral or alkaline
is preferable. In gardens where the soil is acidic it
may be best to grow smaller varieties in pots or
planters, where the soil can be more easily
adjusted if needed. There are three height groups:
dwarf, medium and tall.

China asters are popular annuals because they put
on a bright display when planted in groups.

RECOMMENDED

There are many varieties and cultivars available.

'Pot 'n' Patio' is a popular dwarf cultivar that has
double flowers and grows 6–8" (15–20 cm) tall,
with an equal spread.

GARDENING TIPS

These plants can also be started in peat pots or
peat pellets, because they don't like having their
roots disturbed.

Use the smaller varieties as edging plants and the
taller varieties for cut flower arrangements—tall
varieties may require staking in the garden.

PROBLEMS & PESTS

Aster yellows is a bad problem. Wilt diseases and
aster yellows can be prevented by planting asters in
different locatons each year and by planting resistant varieties. Keep asters away from calendulas,
because they are hosts to insects and disease that
harm asters. Aphids are the most likely insect pests.

*Asters quit blooming when they are cut, but still
make long-lasting cut flowers with a fresh fragrance.
A second sowing in midsummer will provide you
with plants that will bloom into fall or, in a mild
year, into early winter.*

Chrysanthemum

Tricolored Chrysanthemum
Chrysanthemum carinatum

Flower color: Multicolored.
Height: 24" (60 cm). **Spread:** 12" (30 cm).

*I*f you've ever longed for a garden full of blooms to cut and bring indoors, then the tough and dependable blooms of chrysanthemum should be the backbone of your flowerbed. Use them in front of the taller lilies and larkspur and behind the lower-growing mounds of alyssum and lobelia. Their stiff and upright form makes an excellent support system for annual vines, such as black-eyed Susan, or for holding up the more floppy stems of dwarf larkspur or delphinium.

PLANTING

Seeding: Spring and mid-summer.

Planting out: Spring and late summer.

Spacing: 10" (25 cm).

GROWING

These chrysanthemums prefer **full sun** and **tolerate partial shade**. The soil should be **average** and **well drained**.

A second sowing can be made in mid-summer (or purchased plants can be planted out in late summer) for late-season flowers.

These flowers are brightly colored additions to the informal bed or border in their most common shades of red, yellow, white or purple; the centers, petal bases and petal tips are often banded in different colors.

RECOMMENDED

'Court Jesters' has many colors, with the petal bases banded in orange or red.

'Polar Star' has bright white, daisy-like flowers, with an orange band near the petal bases.

Rainbow Series has many colors, with two bands at the petal bases.

GARDENING TIPS

Deadhead to prolong the blooming period.

PROBLEMS & PESTS

Aphids love chrysanthemums and should be washed off with insecticidal soap or a brisk spray from the garden hose.

Chrysanthemums make long-lasting and popular cut flowers. In Victorian flower symbolism, a white chrysanthemum represents truth and a yellow chrysanthemum indicates slighted love.

'Court Jesters'

Cockscomb
Woolflower
Celosia argentea

Flower color: Red, orange, yellow, pink or purple.
Height: 6–36" (15–90 cm), depending on variety. **Spread:** Usually equal to height.

The unusual wrinkled texture of the flowers and the incredible variety of flower forms will make any gardener crow with delight. This annual is great to buy in bloom and give as a gift, perhaps potted up in a novelty container. I once stuck a cockscomb in a clay pot the shape of a chicken and let it nest in the blazing hot sun of a west-facing porch. My children never tired of the intended pun.

PLANTING

Seeding: Indoors in late winter; direct sow in mid- to late spring.

Planting out: Once soil has warmed.

Spacing: Depends on variety.

GROWING

A sheltered spot in **full sun** is best. The soil should be **fertile** and **well drained** with plenty of **organic matter** worked in. Cockscomb likes to be watered regularly.

It is preferable to start plants directly in the garden, but if this can't be done, plant out your early started plants as soon as possible. Their growth becomes stunted when left too long in pots, and they won't adapt to the garden. Seeds should be kept moist while germinating and need to be exposed to light, so they should not be covered. Start the seeds indoors in peat pots or pellets, and plant out cockscomb before it begins to flower.

Use the expected spread of the variety to determine the appropriate spacing. It will usually be between 4" (10 cm) and 18" (45 cm).

Use cockscomb in borders and beds as well as in planters. The flowers are interesting in cut arrangements, either fresh or dried. A mass planting of plume cockscomb is bright and cheerful in the garden. The crested varieties are popular when used as unusual accents and as cut flowers.

RECOMMENDED

Cristata Group (plume cockscomb) has blooms that resemble the combs on roosters. This group also has many varieties and cultivars.

Plumosa Group (plume celosia) has feathery, plume-like blooms. This group has many varieties and cultivars.

'Startrek' has bright pink plumed flowers that radiate out from a central plume.

ALTERNATE SPECIES

C. spicata **'Flamingo'** has spikes of pink flowers that fade to white. It grows about 36" (90 cm) tall.

PROBLEMS & PESTS

Cockscomb may develop root rot if planted out too early or if over-watered when first planted out. Cool, wet weather is the biggest problem.

'Startrek'

To dry the plumes, pick the flowers when they are at their peak and hang them upside down in a cool, shaded place.

Plumosa Group

Coleus

Solenostemon scutellarioides
(also called *Coleus blumei* var. *verschaffeltii*)

Flower color: Light purple; grown as a foliage plant.
Height: 6–36" (15–90 cm). **Spread:** Usually equal to height.

*T*he crown jewel of the annual foliage plants, coleus is much loved as an indoor houseplant and for adding a tropical punch to boring flowerbeds and carefree containers. Coleus is great fun for kids to grow from seed, because each seed packet has several different color combinations. Part of the joy of these striking plants is in watching the foliage patterns develop and taking cuttings to multiply your favorite types.

PLANTING

Seeding: Indoors in winter.

Planting out: Once soil has warmed.

Spacing: 12" (30 cm).

GROWING

Coleus prefers to grow in **light or partial shade**, but it will tolerate full shade if it isn't too dense and full sun if the plants are watered regularly. The soil should be **moist** and **well drained** and of **rich or average fertility**, with lots of **organic matter**.

Place the seeds in a refrigerator for one or two days before planting them on the soil surface. Cold temperatures will assist in breaking their dormancy. They need light to germinate. Seedlings will all be green at first, but leaf variegation will develop as the plants mature.

The colors of the foliage can fade in bright sun, so pick the lighter yellow and gold-leaved varieties for sunny spots. They don't fade as badly. The bold, colorful foliage makes coleus useful grouped together in beds and borders, in mixed containers and as edging plants. Coleus can also be grow indoors as a houseplant in a bright room.

The attractive foliage of this plant is green, red, purple, pink, yellow, bronze or maroon. It is often variegated with two or more colors.

RECOMMENDED

'Carefree' has deeply lobed leaves on dwarf, 10" (25-cm) tall plants.

Wizard Series has large, heart-shaped leaves on compact, 12–14" (30–35-cm) tall plants.

GARDENING TIPS

Coleus is easy to propagate from stem cuttings, and in doing so you can ensure that you have a group of plants with the same leaf markings, shapes or colors.

As your seedlings develop, decide which ones you like best, and when they are about three pairs of leaves high, pinch off the tip. The plants will begin to branch out. Pinch all the tips off regularly as the branches grow. This process will

Coleus can be trained to grow into a standard (tree) form by pinching off the side branches as it grows. Once it reaches the desired height, pinch from the top.

produce a very bushy plant from which you will be able to take a large number of cuttings. The cuttings should be about three leaf pairs long. The cut should be made just below a leaf pair, and then remove the two bottom leaves. Plant the cuttings in pots filled with a soil mix intended for starting seeds. Keep the soil moist but not soggy. The plants should develop roots within a couple of weeks. Because all of the plants are from a single original plant, they will all have the same markings and be of the same color.

When flowerbuds develop, it is best to pinch them off, because the plants tend to stretch out and are less attractive after they have flowered.

PROBLEMS & PESTS
Slugs can destroy foliage in cool weather.

Although coleus is a member of the mint family, with the diagnostic square stems, it has none of the enjoyable culinary or aromatic qualities.

Coreopsis

Coreopsis tinctoria

Flower color: Yellow, red, orange or maroon.
Height: 24–36" (60–90 cm); 8–12" (20–30 cm) for dwarf varieties.
Spread: 8–18" (20–45 cm).

*T*his flower is one that enjoys a good waltz with the breeze. The brightly colored blooms sit high above the fine texture of the foliage on wiry stems to lend a casual, loose feeling to the garden. Use cut coreopsis for golden accents in bouquets of lavender or salvia, or add its warm colors to an arrangement of strawflowers or 'Autumn Joy' sedum.

PLANTING

Seeding: Indoors in mid-winter; direct sow after last frost.

Planting out: After last frost.

Spacing: 8–12" (20–30 cm).

GROWING

Coreopsis prefers **full sun**. The soil should be of **rich or average fertility, light** and **well drained**. Poor soil is also tolerated but with somewhat reduced flowering. Good drainage is the most important factor for these drought-tolerant plants.

Coreopsis looks comfortable growing in front of a rustic wooden fence or repeating in clusters in a bed of perennials. The Tinctoria mix planted with deep purple heuchera or royal purple heliotrope makes a beautiful color combination.

Self-seeding is very possible with these plants, so they may pop up from year to year in the same area if left to their own devices.

Best suited to naturalized meadow plantings, coreopsis can also be used in informal beds and borders where it will flower all season if it is deadheaded regularly. Coreopsis is also a lovely cut flower.

RECOMMENDED

Tinctoria Mixed is bicolored mahogany and gold.

GARDENING TIPS

Coreopsis can be blown over or have its stems broken during heavy rain or high winds. Use twiggy branches for the seedlings to grow between for support. The fine foliage isn't dense enough to hide tomato or peony cages. In very windy spots, it is best to used the dwarf forms.

PROBLEMS & PESTS

Slugs, snails and fungal diseases can be problems.

Cosmos

Cosmos spp.

Flower color: Magenta, rose, pink, purple, white, yellow, orange or scarlet.
Height: 12–84" (30–210 cm). **Spread:** 12–18" (30–45 cm).

O ne summer day in the run-down section of a tiny town, I saw movement through a tall border of cosmos, which was located in an overgrown garden. A stooped and straw-hatted woman, working quietly, made her way through the colorful bed of purple and lavender flowers swaying atop their wiry stems. It is a pleasant summer memory. With their low maintenance and lots of color for little cash, these easy-to-grow cottage garden flowers never fail to delight.

PLANTING

Seeding: Indoors in late winter; direct sow after soil has warmed.

Planting out: After last frost.

Spacing: 12–18" (30–45 cm).

GROWING

Cosmos like to be located in **full sun**. The soil should be of **poor or average fertility** and **well drained**. Cosmos are drought-tolerant. Over-fertilizing and over-watering can reduce the quantity of flowers produced. Yellow cosmos will do better if sown directly in the garden.

Cosmos are useful when mass planted in an informal bed or border. Their height makes them appropriate for planting at the back of a border. They are also attractive in cottage gardens. Keep faded blooms cut to encourage more buds. Often, these plants reseed themselves.

C. bipinnatus

Cut flowers are long lasting and good fillers in arrangements.

C. bipinnatus

'Sea Shells'

RECOMMENDED

C. bipinnatus (annual cosmos) has several cultivars. The flowers come in magenta, rose, pink or white, usually with yellow centers. Old varieties grow 36–72" (90–180 cm) tall, and some cultivars now available grow 12–36" (30–90 cm) tall. One interesting cultivar is **'Sea Shells'** with petals that are rolled into tubes. The plant grows to 36" (90 cm) or taller on long, thin stems.

C. sulphureus (yellow cosmos) has gold, orange, scarlet and yellow flowers. Old varieties grow 7' (2.1 m) tall, and new varieties grow 12–48" (30–120 cm) tall. **Ladybird Series** has compact dwarf plants, 12–14" (30–35 cm) tall, that rarely need staking. The foliage is not as feathered as it is in other cultivars.

GARDENING TIPS

This plant is another one that is likely to need staking but is difficult to stake. Save yourself the trouble of staking by planting it in a sheltered location or against a fence. You could also grow shorter varieties. If staking can't be avoided, push twiggy branches into the ground when the plants are young and allow them to grow up between the branches to provide support. The branches will be hidden by the mature plants.

PROBLEMS & PESTS

Cosmos rarely has any problems, but watch for wilt, aster yellows, powdery mildew and aphids.

The name cosmos is from Greek and means 'beautiful.'

Creeping Zinnia

Sanvitalia procumbens

Flower color: Yellow or orange with dark brown or purple centers.
Height: 4–8" (10–20 cm). **Spread:** 12–18" (30–46 cm).

The narrow leaves and small but numerous daisy-form flowers of creeping zinnia made a spectacular groundcover on a mound of sandy soil at the entrance to a housing development one summer. Soon, the homeowners imitated the success at their entrance by adding creeping zinnias to the dry, sandy soil around their mailboxes and in their south-facing flowerbeds, where other flowers had dried out. You can also add creeping zinnias to hanging baskets, and combine them with other flowers that prefer dry conditions, such as verbena and portulaca.

PLANTING

Seeding: Direct sow in mid-spring.

Spacing: 12" (30 cm).

GROWING

Creeping zinnias prefer **full sun**. The soil should be of **average fertility** and **light, sandy** and **well drained**. Creeping zinnias can be used as annual groundcovers, edging plants, in hanging baskets and in mixed containers.

Do not cover the seeds when you sow them because they need light to germinate.

RECOMMENDED

'**Sprite**' is a mounding plant, 8" (20 cm) tall with yellow-orange flowers with dark centers.

'**Yellow Carpet**' is a low-growing dwarf plant that is up to 4" (10 cm) tall and 18" (46 cm) wide. It has bright yellow flowers with dark centers.

PROBLEMS & PESTS

Keep zinnias from getting hit by a sprinkler system, or you'll have mildew and fungal problems.

Creeping zinnias are one of the easiest annuals to grow. They are also one of the easiest to damage with too much care—over-watering and over-fertilizing can quickly kill the plants. The less you do, the better creeping zinnias will do.

Cup Flower

Nierembergia caerulea (also called *N. hippomanica*)

Flower color: Blue, purple or white.
Height: 6–12" (15–30 cm). **Spread:** 6–12" (15–30 cm).

You may pout and complain over cool summer weather, but this happy little annual will put out a cheerful display when the weather is cool and gray. Let the low-mounding habit of this plant spill over pathways in the front of your border, or let the cup-like blossoms drip from hanging baskets. Dainty and demure up close, where the shape can be admired, these flowers are outstanding when grouped with other cool-season annuals, such as pansies and fuchsias.

PLANTING

Seeding: Indoors in mid-winter; in mild climates, direct sow in sheltered locations in mid-fall.

Planting out: Spring.

Spacing: 6–12" (15–30 cm).

GROWING

Cup flower grows well in **full sun** or **partial shade**. The soil should be **fertile, moist** and **well drained**.

Use cup flower as an annual groundcover plant. It is also useful for edging beds and borders, in rock walls and rock gardens and in containers and hanging baskets. It grows best when summers are cool, and it can withstand a light frost.

Cup flower is a perennial used as an annual. It is marginally hardy along the coast, and in an exceptionally mild year it may survive winter.

RECOMMENDED

'Mont Blanc' has white flowers with yellow centers.

'Purple Robe' has deep purple flowers with golden eyes.

GARDENING TIPS

In the warmest areas of the Pacific Northwest, cup flower may survive the winter with protection, but this plant is quick to grow from seed. Growing new plants may prove easier than protecting mature plants over winter.

PROBLEMS & PESTS

Slugs and snails are likely to be the worst problem for these plants. Because cup flowers are susceptible to tobacco mosaic virus, don't plant them near any flowering tobacco or tomato plants.

'Mont Blanc'

The former species name hippomanica *is from Greek and means 'drives horses crazy.' Whether they went crazy because they loved to eat it or from actually eating the plant is unsure.*

Cup-and-Saucer Vine
Cathedral Bells
Cobaea scandens

Flower color: Purple or white.
Height: 15–25' (4.5–7.5 m) in hot summer areas; 6' (1.8 m) in cool summer areas.
Spread: May vary.

*N*ow here's a lovely summer-blooming vine that sounds just like it's common name—the cup-shaped blooms are backed by a disc-like saucer. This dainty vine is perfect for draping up the side of a porch or climbing up a trellis to screen a summer patio, or for adding Victorian charm to a summer tea party.

PLANTING

Seeding: Indoors in mid-winter.

Planting out: After last frost.

Spacing: 12" (30 cm).

GROWING

Cup-and-saucer vine prefers **full sun**. The soil should be **well drained** and of **average fertility**. Grow up a trellis, over an arbor or along a chain-link fence. Cup-and-saucer vine requires a sturdy support in order to climb. It uses grabbing hooks to climb so won't be able to grow up a wall without something to grab hold of.

Set the seeds on edge when planting them, and barely cover them with soil.

GARDENING TIPS

This plant is fond of hot weather and will do best if planted in a sheltered site with southern exposure. It can be trained to fill almost any space.

PROBLEMS & PESTS

This plant may have trouble with aphids.

Cup-and-saucer vine is a perennial that is grown as an annual. Where it is grown as a perennial, it may eventually reach heights of 30–70' (9–21 m).

This interesting vine has sweet-scented flowers that are a cream color with a green tinge when they open; the flowers darken to purple as they age.

Dahlberg Daisy

Golden Fleece

Thymophylla tenuiloba (also called *Dyssodia tenuiloba*)

Flower color: Yellow or less commonly orange.
Height: 8–12" (20–30 cm). **Spread:** 12" (30 cm).

The yellow daisy form of this delightful little flower is a favorite with novice gardeners. Its adaptability to poor, sandy soils makes it perfect for draping over the boulders of a rock garden or growing in the often hostile environment of a parking strip. The foliage adds a fine and lacy frill to hanging baskets or container gardens. Use it with the contrasting foliage of sedums or succulents that also tolerant of bright sun and sandy soil.

PLANTING

Seeding: Indoors in mid-winter; direct sow in spring.

Planting out: After last frost.

Spacing: 8–12" (20–30 cm).

GROWING

Plant Dahlberg daisy in **full sun.** Any **well-drained** soil is suitable, although soil of **poor or average fertility** is preferred. Dahlberg daisy prefers cool summers. In hot summer climates, it is a spring-flowering annual.

Direct-sown plants may not flower until quite late in summer. For earlier blooms, start the seeds indoors. Don't cover the seeds, because they require light to germinate. These attractive plants may self-sow to reappear each year.

These plants are versatile for use in edging borders, planted along the tops of rock walls or in mixed containers or hanging baskets. Any location where they can cascade over and trail down an edge will look wonderful.

GARDENING TIPS

If you trim the plants back when flowering seems to be slowing, it will encourage new growth and more blooms.

Dahlberg daisy has fragrant foliage that some people compare to a lemon-thyme scent, which may be connected to the botanical name Thymophylla, *meaning thyme-leaf.*

Dahlia

Dahlia spp.

Flower color: Purple, pink, white, yellow, orange, red or bicolored.
Height: 8–24" (20–60 cm); up to 5' (1.5 m) for some varieties.
Spread: 8–18" (20–45 cm).

*D*warf dahlias may be the perfect bedding plant—non-stop flowers held on stiff upright stems in a paintbox array of colors, with blooms in double, semi-double and bicolored forms. Contrast the chubby, rounded flowers with the slender blooms of glads or a graceful skirt of alyssum. The tall dahlias look regal and formal in the back of a bed and thrive when grown in the reflected heat of a stone or brick wall. Fill a large pot with dahlias and you will enjoy a multitude of colors throughout summer.

PLANTING

Seeding: Indoors in mid- to late winter; direct sow in spring.

Planting out: After last frost.

Spacing: 12" (30 cm).

GROWING

Dahlias prefer **full sun**. The soil should be **fertile, rich in organic matter, moist** and **well drained**. Tubers can also be purchased and started early indoors. Dahlias are perennials that are treated like annuals. Their tubers can be lifted in fall, dried and stored over winter in slightly moist peat moss. They may even survive a very mild winter outdoors if they are given a thick mulch once the foliage has died back.

Dahlia flowers are categorized by size, from giants with blooms over 10" (25 cm) in diameter to mignons with blooms up to 2" (5 cm) in diameter. They are then categorized by shape. A few examples of flower types are peony, formal and informal decorative, semi-cactus and waterlily.

Semi-cactus type

Waterlily type

Peony type 'Bishop of Llandaff'

Informal decorative type

Informal decorative type

Dahlias make attractive and colorful additions to a mixed border. The smaller varieties make good edging plants and the larger ones make good shrub replacement plants, useful for filling in large areas for summer. The special varieties with unusual or interestingly formed flowers are attractive as specimen plants.

RECOMMENDED

'Bishop of Llandaff' has miniature, peony-type, red flowers with dark centers. The foliage is purple.

'Piccolo' has early single blooms in many bright colors. The compact plants grow 8" (20 cm) tall.

'Redskin' has bronze foliage and miniature double flowers in many colors. The plants grow up to 24" (60 cm) tall, with an equal spread.

Formal decorative type

GARDENING TIPS

If there is a particular size, color or form of dahlia that you want, it is best to start them from tubers of that type. Seed-grown dahlias show a great deal of variation in color and form, because the seed is generally sold in mixed packages.

In order to keep dahlias blooming and attractive it is essential to remove the spent blooms.

PROBLEMS & PESTS

There are a few problems a dahlia grower may encounter: aphids, powdery mildew, slugs and earwigs are the most likely. If a worse problem afflicts your dahlias, it may be easier to destroy the infected plants and start over.

Informal decorative

Dusty Miller

Senecio cineraria

Flower color: Yellow or white; foliage is silvery.
Height: Usually about 12" (30 cm); can grow to 24" (60 cm).
Spread: Width is usually equal to height or slightly narrower.

*T*he silver leaves makes this a framing plant for your flowers. Use dusty miller around deep purple heliotrope, bright pink geraniums and sky blue ageratum, and you will see how the flower colors pop out and sing from their silver frame. Dusty miller often survives winter, but the silver leaves will look weary and tarnished. Treat these flowers as annuals and start each spring with fresh plants. Dusty miller will put the spotlight on your flowerbed stars all summer long.

PLANTING

Seeding: Indoors in mid-winter.

Planting out: Spring.

Spacing: 12" (30 cm).

GROWING

Dusty Miller prefers **full sun** but will tolerate light shade. The soil should be of **average fertility** and **well drained**. These plants can withstand some frost, and they may overwinter in a mild year.

The soft, silvery, lacy leaves of this plant are its main feature, and it is used primarily as an edging plant. It is also used in beds, borders and containers. The silvery foliage makes a good backdrop to show off the brightly colored flowers of other plants.

'Silver Dust'

'Cirrus'

RECOMMENDED

'Cirrus' has lobed, silvery green or white foliage.

'Silver Dust' has deeply lobed, silvery white foliage.

'Silver Lace' has delicate, silvery white foliage that glows in the moonlight.

GARDENING TIPS

Pinch off the flowers before they bloom or they will detract from the foliage.

PROBLEMS & PESTS

Dusty Miller is usually problem free, although it may occasionally suffer from rust. It is best to remove afflicted plants and not attempt to grow them again in the same location.

Dwarf Morning Glory
Convolvulus tricolor

Flower color: Blue, purple or pink.
Height: 12–16" (30–40 cm). **Spread:** 9–12" (23–30 cm).

*L*illiputian blooms on compact, low-growing plants are perfect for close-up viewing. These flowers are the ones to plant as soon as you move into a new garden, because they don't need fertile or well-worked soil, and they learn to adapt to poor growing conditions. They can also be enjoyed when paired with other drapers in a hanging basket, preferably hung at eye level so that visitors can look right into the trumpet-shaped blooms. The petals are edged in rich, dark colors surrounding a stunning yellow eye, which closes after nightfall when the petals fold the flower shut.

PLANTING

Seeding: Indoors in late winter; direct sow in mid- or late spring.

Planting out: Mid- or late spring.

Spacing: 8–12" (20–30 cm).

GROWING

Dwarf morning glories prefer **full sun**. The soil should be of **poor or average fertility** and **well drained**. These plants may not flower well in rich, moist soil.

Soak the seeds in water overnight before planting them. If starting seeds early indoors, use peat pots to avoid root damage when transplanting.

Grow these compact, mounding plants in containers, hanging baskets, rock walls and borders.

RECOMMENDED

Ensign Series has low-growing spreading plants growing 6' (15 cm) tall. **'Royal Ensign'** has deep blue flowers with white and yellow throats.

'Royal Ensign'

This daytime bloomer has flowers that last only a single day, blooming in the morning and twisting shut that evening.

'Royal Ensign'

Fan Flower

Scaevola aemula

Flower color: Blue or purple.
Height: Up to 8" (20 cm). **Spread:** Up to 4' (1.2 m).

*A*n antique wicker plant stand on a sunny front porch should be easy to fill with flowers, but it took several summers before I discovered fan flower as the perfect heat-tolerant draper with summer-long blooms. Looking like a giant lobelia, but with thick, fleshy leaves, fan flower cools any hot spot with waves of blue and is forgiving if you forget to water it—it may be wilted but will recover quickly once you give it a drink.

Fan flower is native to Australia and Polynesia.

PLANTING

Seeding: Indoors in late winter.

Planting out: After last frost.

Spacing: 24–48" (60–120 cm).

GROWING

Fan flower grows equally well in **full sun** or **light shade**. The soil should be of **average fertility, moist** and **well drained**. Water regularly, because these plants don't like to completely dry out.

Fan flower is a very popular plant for use in hanging baskets and containers, but it can also be used along the tops of rock walls and in rock gardens where it can trail downwards. This plant can also make an interesting addition to mixed borders or under shrubs where the long, trailing stems form an attractive groundcover.

These attractive plants are actually perennials that are too tender to survive winter. They can be brought in over winter and kept in a bright room or, during summer, cuttings can be taken and the new plants can be grow indoors to be used the following summer. Seeds can be difficult to find.

RECOMMENDED

'Blue Wonder' has long branches that trail, making it ideal for hanging baskets. It can eventually spread 36" (90 cm) or more wide.

'Saphira' is a new compact variety, with deep blue flowers. It spreads about 12" (30 cm) wide.

GARDENING TIPS

Fan flower responds well to pinching and trimming. Frequently pinching the tips or trimming the entire plant back will keep it bushy and blooming.

PROBLEMS & PESTS

This plant may get whitefly if it becomes stressed from lack of water.

Forget-Me-Not
Myosotis sylvatica

Flower color: Blue, pink or white.
Height: 6–12" (15–30 cm). **Spread:** 6" (15 cm) or wider.

*T*he best flower in the garden for teaching little ones about plant names, this country charmer will pop up year after year, so it has earned its common name and easy-to-grow reputation. Use forget-me-nots as a cover planting in a bed of tulips or daffodils, or let it reseed itself alongside a wood-land path. It has the casual form of a wild-flower, with the true blue color of a pedigree annual.

Forget-me-not is a delightful addition to woodland or wet areas and a great companion to wildflower and native plant gardens.

PLANTING

Seeding: Direct sow in fall or early spring.

Spacing: 10" (25 cm).

GROWING

Forget-me-not prefers **light or partial shade,** but it will tolerate full sun if the weather isn't too hot. The soil should be **fertile, moist** and **well drained**. Adding lots of organic matter to the soil will help it retain moisture while maintaining good drainage. This flower reseeds easily and thrives in cooler parts of the garden.

Seeds sown in fall will flower in early spring, and seeds sown in spring will flower in summer or fall. Forget-me-not is a short-lived perennial that is treated like an annual.

Forget-me-not can be used in the front of flower-beds or to edge beds and borders, in mixed containers and in rock gardens and walls. You can also mix it with naturalized spring-flowering bulbs.

RECOMMENDED

Ball Series has compact, mound-forming plants with flowers in several colors.

PROBLEMS & PESTS

Slugs and snails may be troublesome. Downy mildew, powdery mildew and rust may also cause occasional trouble.

The name comes from the way this biennial lives a short life after blooming but then reappears as new seedlings all over the garden.

Four-O' Clock Flower

Mirabilis jalapa

Flower color: Red, pink, magenta, yellow, white or bicolored.
Height: 18–36" (45–90 cm). **Spread:** 18–24" (45–60 cm).

*T*his flower likes to put on a show. Not an early riser, four-o'clock flower waits until late afternoon, when the common posies are wilting in the hot sun, to open its petals ever so slowly to show off trumpet-shaped blooms. The sweet fragrance that fills summer nights is this flower's encore.

PLANTING

Seeding: Indoors in late winter; direct sow in mid-spring.

Planting out: Mid-spring.

Spacing: 16–24" (40–60 cm).

GROWING

Four-o'clock flower prefers **full sun** but will tolerate partial shade. The soil should be **fertile**, though any **well-drained** soil will be tolerated.

This plant may be grown from tuberous roots. Dig and store roots in fall and replant in spring to enjoy larger plants. This plant is a perennial that is treated as an annual.

This plant can be used in beds and borders, containers and window boxes. The flowers are scented, so they are often planted near deck patios or terraces where their scent can be enjoyed in the afternoon and evening.

PROBLEMS & PESTS

This plant has very few problems as long as it is given well-drained soil.

Many species of moths are attracted to the flowers of this plant, which may bloom in several colors on a single plant.

Fuchsia

Fuchsia x *hybrida*

Flower color: Pink, red, purple or white; often bicolored.
Height: 6–36" (15–90 cm) **Spread:** 8–36" (20–90 cm)

Fuchsia flowers never fail to ignite the imagination and liven the garden with old-fashioned elegance. The cool summer areas of the Pacific Northwest are perfect fuchsia growing climates, but these beautiful shade-blooming plants should be grown in every garden. Dripping from baskets, spilling from rockeries or flowering from container gardens, fuchsias are our reward for putting up with cloudy summer days. Pair the bi-colored blooms with the fine-textured flowers of lobelia or the more upright blooms of impatiens for color combos made for the shade. The mostly pink and red fuchsia blooms also make a loud but happy match with the crazy quilt patterns of wine-colored coleus or a quieter combination with cool white and green foliage plants.

Children, and some adults, enjoy popping the fat buds of fuchsia. The temptation to squeeze them is irresistable.

PLANTING

Seeding: Not recommended.

Planting out: After last frost.

Spacing: 12–24" (30–60 cm).

GROWING

Fuchsias are grown in **partial or light shade**. They are not tolerant of summer heat and full sun can be too hot for them. Soil should be **fertile, moist** and **well drained**.

'Deep Purple'

The upright fuchsias grow 18–36" (45–90 cm) tall. They can be used in mixed planters, beds and borders. The pendulous fuchsias grow 6–24" (15–60 cm) tall. They are most often used in hanging baskets but make attractive additions to planters and rock gardens where the flowers dangle from the flexible branches.

Fuchsias can be started from seed, although the germination rate can be poor and erratic. If you are up for a challenge then start the plants indoors in mid-winter. Ensure that the soil is warm—at 68–75° F (20–24° C). Seeds can take from two weeks to two months to sprout. Plants will only start to flower when the days have more than 13 hours of light. It may be late in summer before you see any reward for your efforts.

Although fuchsias are hard to start from seed, they are easy to propagate from cuttings. Snip off 6" (15 cm) of new tip growth, remove the leaves from the lower third of the stem and insert the cuttings into soft soil or perlite. Once rooted and potted up, the plants will bloom all summer.

'Snowburner'

RECOMMENDED

There are dozens of cultivars of fuchsia, of which the following are just a few examples.

'Deep Purple' has purple petals and white sepals.

'Snowburner' has white petals and pink sepals.

'Swingtime' has white petals that are pink at the bases and pink sepals. The plant grows 12–24" (30–60 cm) tall, with a spread about 6" (15 cm) wider. They can be grown in a hanging basket or as relaxed upright plants in beds and borders.

'Winston Churchill' has purple petals and pink sepals. The plant grows 18–30" (20–75 cm) tall, with an equal spread. The plant is quite upright in form but is often grown in hanging baskets.

GARDENING TIPS

Fuchsias are perennials that are grown as annuals. In the warmest locations along the coast they can survive winter if left in the garden with a good mulch. Gardeners in other parts of the region will have to bring the plants indoors if they want to keep them for the following summer. To store fuchsias over the winter, cut back the plants to 6" (15 cm) stumps after the first light frost and place them in a dark, cold, but not freezing, location. A garage, basement or crawl space will work fine. Water just enough to keep the soil barely moist and do not feed. In mid-spring, repot the naked stumps, set them near a bright window and fertilize them lightly. You can set your over-wintered plants outdoors after all danger of frost is past.

When deadheading or removing the spent blossoms of fuchsias, be sure to pluck the swollen seedpods from behind the fading petals. Without removing the pods, the seeds will ripen and rob the plant of energy necessary for further flower production.

Fuchsias bloom on new growth and prefer a high nitrogen plant food that encourages new growth.

Fuchsia need to be well watered, particularly if they are growing in a hot location or in full sun. Ensure that the soil has good drainage or they can develop rot problems if left to sit in excess water. Fuchsias planted in well-aerated soil with plenty of perlite are almost impossible to overwater. As summer wears on, increase the amount of water given to the plants as the pots and baskets fill with thirsty roots.

PROBLEMS & PESTS

Common insect pests are aphids, spider mites and whiteflies. Diseases like crown rot, root rot and rust can be avoided with good air circulation and drainage.

Some gardeners who have kept their fuchsias over several years have trained this plant to adopt a tree form.

Gazania
Gazania rigens

Flower color: Red, orange, yellow, pink or cream.
Height: Usually 6–8" (15–20 cm); it may reach heights of 12–18" (30–45 cm).
Spread: 8–12" (20–30 cm).

I first admired the hardy nature of this daisy-like flower when I saw it blooming in a parking strip between the sidewalk and the street. The summer sun was bright, but gazania bloomed even brighter, and the mat of foliage and flowers was so thick that not a single weed could hope to wedge in. The silvery gray foliage of this annual frames the brightly colored petals, which often have contrasting stripes of color running along them or in bands marking their bases.

PLANTING

Seeding: Indoors in late winter; direct sow after last frost.

Planting out: After last frost.

Spacing: 6–10" (15–25 cm).

GROWING

Gazania grows best in **full sun** but tolerates partial shade. The soil should be of **poor to average fertility, sandy** and **well drained**. This plant grows best in hot weather over 80° F (27° C). There is a good chance that your gazania may survive winter. This plant is a perennial that is treated as an annual in most of North America. However, along the mild Pacific coast it is often hardy and can continue blooming up until the first frost.

Low-growing gazania makes an excellent groundcover and is also useful for edging beds, exposed slopes and mixed containers.

RECOMMENDED

'Daybreak' flowers have bright contrasting stripes down the centers of the petals.

'Moonglow' has yellow, double flowers that will stay open on cloudy days.

PROBLEMS & PESTS

Over-watering is the likely cause of any problems encountered by gazania.

Flowers close in cloudy weather and at night. This clue can be helpful in predicting rainy weather.

Geranium

Pelargonium spp.

Flower color: Red, pink, violet, orange, salmon, white or purple.
Height: 12–24" (30–60 cm). **Spread:** 12–48" (30–120 cm).

*T*hese flowers are a true classic, whether you use red geraniums in clay pots or pink geraniums with variegated ivy in window boxes. Despite the traditional displays, you can be imaginative with this easy-to-grow standard. Use ivy geraniums in plum and purples to add drama to a bed of tropical colors or white geraniums to accent a garden of silver and gray plants. Pot bright orange geraniums along with the wild quilt colors of coleus for an eye-catching array.

PLANTING

Seeding: Indoors in early winter; direct sow in spring.

Planting out: After last frost.

Spacing: Zonal geraniums, about 12" (30 cm); ivy-leaved geraniums, 24–36" (60–90 cm).

P. zonale

GROWING

Geraniums prefer **full sun**, but they will tolerate partial shade, although they may not bloom as profusely. The soil should be **fertile** and **well drained**. Geraniums are perennials that are treated like annuals. They can be kept indoors over winter in a bright room.

Plants are slow to come from seed so purchasing plants may prove easier. However, if you would like to try starting your own from seed they should be started indoors in early winter and covered with clear plastic until they germinate to maintain humidity. Transplant seedlings into individual 3–4" (8–10 cm) pots once they have three or four leaves. They need lots of light to maintain compact shape. Keep them in bright locations in your house.

Edema is an unusual condition to which geraniums are susceptible. This disease occurs when a plant is over-watered and the leaf cells burst. A warty surface develops on the leaves. There is no cure, although it can be avoided through careful watering and, as the plant grows, any damaged leaves can be removed. The condition is more common in ivy-leaved geraniums.

P. pelatum

Deadheading is essential to keep geraniums in bloom and looking neat. The flowerheads are attached to long stems that break off easily where they attach to the plant.

Geraniums are one of the most popular annual plants. Use zonal geraniums in beds, borders and containers. Ivy-leaved geraniums are most often used in hanging baskets and containers to take advantage of the trailing habit, but they are also interesting when used as bedding plants where they form a bushy, spreading groundcover.

P. zonale

RECOMMENDED

The following species and varieties are some of
the easier ones to start from seed. Many popular
varieties can only be propagated from cuttings
and so, must be purchased as plants.

P. peltatum (ivy-leaved geranium) grows up
to 12" (30 cm) tall and up to 4' (1.2 m) wide.
A wide range of colors are available. **Summer
Showers Series** is one of the first mixtures of seed
available for ivy-leaved geraniums. These flowers
can take four or more months to flower from
seed. **Tornado Series** is very good for hanging
baskets and containers. The plants are quite
compact, and the flowers are either lilac or white.

P. zonale (zonal geranium) grows up to 24"
(60 cm) tall and 12" (30 cm) wide. Dwarf
varieties grow up to 8" (20 cm) tall and 5"
(13 cm) wide. The flowers are red, pink, purple,
orange or white. **Pinto Series** is available in all
colors, and seed is generally sold by the color so
you don't have to purchase a mixed packet and
hope you like the colors you get. **Orbit Series**
has attractive early-blooming, compact plants,
but the seed is often sold in a mixed packet.
Some individual colors are available.

PROBLEMS & PESTS

Aphids will flock to over-fertilized plants, but
they can usually be washed off before they do
much damage. Leaf spot and blight may bother
geraniums growing in cool, moist soil.

P. zonale

*Ivy-leaved geraniums
are one of the most
beautiful plants to
include in a mixed
hanging basket.*

P. zonale

Gerbera Daisy
Transvaal Daisy
Gerbera jamesonii

Flower color: Pink, purple, red, orange or yellow; in bright or pastel shades.
Height: 8–18" (20–45 cm). **Spread:** Up to 24" (60 cm).

*T*hese oversized, daisy-style flowers bloom in bright cartoon colors, making gerbera daisies the perfect annual for gardeners with a sense of humor. The most memorable display I ever saw had three old paint cans used as planters. There was one can of yellow daisies, one of orange and one of red, and each can had paint of the same color dripping down the sides. Pair gerberas up with contrasting, spiky flowers of a salvia, or use low, ground-covering mats of creeping thyme. If you have a small pot with only room for one plant, make the solitary choice a gerbera daisy and you'll really make a statement.

PLANTING

Seeding: Not recommended.

Planting out: Late spring.

Spacing: 18" (45 cm).

GROWING

Gerbera daisies prefer **full sun** but will tolerate partial shade. The soil should be **well drained** and have **plenty of organic matter** worked in and be of **average to high fertility.** These daisies prefer warm weather. In the garden they make an impressive addition to annual beds and borders as well as in mixed containers.

These plants can be quite difficult to grow and are slow to develop from seed. It may prove easier to purchase plants in spring. If you want to attempt to grow gerbera daisies from seed, use only very fresh seed, because it loses viability very quickly. When seeding indoors, start them in December or January and cover the seed flat or pot with clear plastic to maintain high humidity while the seeds are germinating. When planting out, be careful not to plant too deeply.

Gerbera daisies make popular houseplants.

Gerberas are popular and best known for their use as cut flowers. For longer lasting flowers, slit the bottoms of the stems upwards 1" (2.5 cm) to help them absorb water.

RECOMMENDED

'California Giants' grows to 24" (60 cm) tall, with flowers in red, orange, yellow and pink.

'Happipot' has compact plants that grow to 8" (20 cm) tall, with mixed flower colors.

'Skipper' has smaller leaves and shorter stems and grows 8–10" (20–25 cm) tall. It is good for edging beds or for containers.

PROBLEMS & PESTS

Crown and root rots are the most common problems. Also watch out for leafminers, aphids, thrips and whiteflies.

Globe Amaranth

Gomphrena globosa

Flower color: Purple, pink, white or sometimes red.
Height: 6–24" (15–60 cm). **Spread:** 6–12" (15–30 cm).

*L*ike fluffy pom-poms dancing in the breeze, this globe-shaped flower will inspire plenty of craft projects. Grow these easy-to-dry flowers with other plants that provide material for dry arrangements, such as statice and strawflowers. Planted in a rustic half-barrel planter or alongside an old wooden fence, these unusual flower balls will bestow excitement into any landscape. For an unusual display, pair globe amaranth's clover-like blooms with the silver gray foliage of the lacy-leaved dusty miller or the tropical-colored coleus.

PLANTING

Seeding: Indoors in late winter.

Planting out: After last frost.

Spacing: 10" (25 cm).

GROWING

Globe amaranth prefers **full sun**. The soil should be of **average fertility** and **well drained**. This plant likes hot weather. When seeding, seeds will germinate quicker if soaked for two to four days before sowing. They need warm soil above 70° F (21° C) to sprout.

Globe amaranth forms a rounded, bushy plant that is dotted with papery, clover-like flowers. Use it in an informal or cottage garden.

These plants are underused because they don't start flowering until later in summer compared to many other annuals. Don't overlook them—they are worth the wait and provide color from mid-summer until the first frost.

RECOMMENDED

Buddy Series has more compact plants, 6–12" (15–30 cm) tall, with deep purple flowers.

ALTERNATE SPECIES

'Strawberry Fields' is a hybrid with bright orange-red flowers. It grows about 30" (75 cm) tall and spreads about half as much.

PROBLEMS & PESTS

Globe amaranth is susceptible to some fungal diseases, such as gray mold and leaf spot.

Globe amaranth flowers are popular for cutting and drying because they keep their color and form well when dried.

If you want to pick and dry the flowers, it is best to do so before they are completely open. Hang them upside down in a cool, dry location to dry.

Godetia
Satin Flower
Clarkia amoena (also called *Godetia amoena* or *G. grandiflora*)

Flower color: Pink, red- to purple-toned, or white; some bicolored.
Height: 12–36" (30–90 cm). **Spread:** 10–18" (25–45 cm).

The fragile-looking petals on godetia have a satin-like luster, which belies the fact that they will survive in some pretty tough situations. I have seen this local native growing out of poor, rocky soil in desert-like heat. The shiny sheen on the petals seemed to shimmer in the sunlight. The flowers are large enough to stand out in a crowd, but soft enough to mix well with fine-textured rock garden plants such as thyme and various succulents.

PLANTING

Seeding: Direct sow in spring or late summer.

Spacing: Slightly crowded.

GROWING

Godetia will grow equally well in **full sun or light shade**. The soil should be **well drained, light, sandy** and of **poor or average fertility**. These plants don't like to be over-watered, so be sure to let them dry out between waterings. They do well in cool weather. Start in garden in spring for summer bloom and in late summer for fall bloom. Seed plants where you want them to grow, because they are difficult to transplant. Starting seeds indoors is not recommended.

When caring for your garden, thin young plants so they are 6–12" (15–30 cm) apart. These flowers are useful in beds, borders, containers and rock gardens. The flowers can be used for fresh arrangements.

RECOMMENDED

Satin Series has compact plants that grow 8–12" (20–30 cm) tall. The single flowers come in many colors, including some bicolors.

PROBLEMS & PESTS

Root rot can occur in poorly drained soil.

This plant produces gorgeous showy flowers despite its preference for poor soil.

'Satin Series'

Heliotrope

Cherry Pie Plant

Heliotropium aborscens

Flower color: Shades of purple; white is rare.
Height: 8–24" (20–60 cm). **Spread:** 12–24" (30–60 cm).

Walking through a nursery one summer day, I was overtaken by a delicious aroma. Looking up I saw a basket of royal purple blooms—heliotrope, the source of the fragrance. It is easy to smell why, in some parts of the country, heliotrope is called cherry pie plant. Pair it in hanging baskets with other sun-lovers, such as bacopa and petunias, or use the deep purple blooms in patio pots with pink petunias and purple ivy geraniums. Design a fragrance garden with heliotrope, sweet peas, stock, snapdragons and lemon thyme for a summer of aromatherapy.

These old-fashioned flowers may have been popular in your grandmother's garden. Their recent come-back is not surprise owing to their attractive foliage, flowers and scent.

PLANTING

Seeding: Indoors in mid-winter.

Planting out: Once soil has warmed.

Spacing: 12–18" (30–45 cm).

GROWING

Heliotrope grows best in **full sun**. The soil should be **fertile, rich in organic matter, moist** and **well drained**. Heliotrope is ideal for growing in containers or in beds near windows and patios where the wonderful scent can be enjoyed with ease.

RECOMMENDED

'Dwarf Marine' or **'Mini Marine'** is a compact, bushy plant with fragrant, purple flowers. It grows 8–12" (20–30 cm) tall and is a good winter houseplant.

'Marine' has violet blue flowers and grows to be about 18" (45 cm) tall.

GARDENING TIPS

These plants can be pinched and shaped as you please. A tree form can be created by pinching off the lower branches as it grows until it reaches the height you desire; then the top can be pinched and the plant encouraged to bush out. A shorter, bushy form is most popular. Pinch all the tips that develop to encourage the plant to bush out at ground level.

These plants can be grown indoors as houseplants in a sunny window, and outdoor plants can be moved indoors for winter flowers. The plants may survive for years if kept outdoors all summer and indoors all winter in a cool, bright room.

PROBLEMS & PESTS

Aphids and whiteflies can be problems.

Plants that are a little on the underwatered side tend to have a stronger scent.

'Marine'

Impatiens

Impatiens spp.

Flower color: Shades of purple, red, pink, orange, white or bicolored.
Height: 6–36" (15–90 cm). **Spread:** 12–24" (30–60 cm).

*P*illows of impatiens with one color blending into the other as the mounds grow taller and wider all summer long are a popular choice for city flowerbeds. Use this easy-to-grow annual in unusual ways to show off its versatility. A hollowed-out fallen log can be planted with pink impatiens in the woodland garden, or a row of white impatiens can line the walkway in a formal garden. For gardeners that want a tropical look to their flowerbeds, the bright neon colors of the New Guinea impatiens never fail to open eyes and turn up the volume in gardens that want a party atmosphere.

PLANTING

Seeding: Indoors in mid-winter; balsam impatiens in late winter.

Planting out: Once soil has warmed.

Spacing: 12–18" (30–45 cm).

I. balsalmia

GROWING

All impatiens will do best in **partial shade** but will tolerate full shade or, if kept moist, full sun. New Guinea and balsam impatiens are best adapted to sunny locations. The soil should be **fertile, humus-rich, moist** and **well drained.** When seeding, don't cover seeds—they germinate best when exposed to light.

Busy Lizzie is best known for its ability to grow and flower profusely in even the deepest shade. Mass plant in beds under trees, along shady fences or walls, in porch planters or hanging baskets.

When the seedpods are almost ripe, the lightest touch will cause them to explode and spew their seeds.

I. walleriana

New Guinea impatiens are almost shrubby in form and are popular in patio planters, beds and borders. They will grow well in full sun and may not flower as profusely in deep shade. They are grown as much for their variegated leaves as for their flowers.

Balsam impatiens were popular garden plants in the Victorian era and are experiencing a comeback in popularity. Their habit is more upright than the other two impatiens, and they are attractive when grouped in beds and borders.

RECOMMENDED

New impatiens varieties are introduced every year, expanding the selection of size, form and color. The following are a few that are popular year after year.

New Guinea Group (New Guinea impatiens) grow 12–24" (30–60 cm) tall and 12" (30 cm) or

New Guinea Group

The name impatien corresponds to the impatient nature of the seedpods. When ripe, the seedpods burst open with the slightest touch and scatter their seeds.

wider. The flowers come in shades of red, orange, pink, purple or white. **'Tango'** is the most common variety to grow from seed. The compact plants grow to 12–18" (30–45 cm) tall and wide and have orange flowers.

I. balsamina (balsam impatiens) grows 12–36" (30–90 cm) tall and up to 18" (45 cm) wide. The flowers comes in shades of purple, red, pink or white. There are several double-flowered cultivars, such as **'Camellia-flowered'** or **'Topknot.'**

I. walleriana (busy Lizzie) grows 6–18" (15–45 cm) tall and up to 24" (60 cm) wide. These flowers come in shades of red, orange, pink, purple, white or bicolored. **Super Elfin Series** is a common group of cultivars. The flowers are available in many shades, including bicolors. The compact plants grow about 12" (30 cm) tall, but they may spread more. **'Victoria Rose'** is an award-winning cultivar, with its deep pink, double or semi-double flowers.

New Guinea Group

I. walleriana

Licorice Plant

Helichrysum petiolare

Flower color: Yellowish white. **Height:** 20" (50 cm).
Spread: About 36" (90 cm); sometimes up to 6' (1.8 m).

*T*he carefree gardener will find licorice plant easy to love because frosty weather, rain storms, heat waves and even browsing deer and sneaky slugs won't destroy this tough plant. The matte finish of the fuzzy gray or lime green foliage and lack of flowers make licorice plant a perfect backdrop for both pastel or brightly colored flowers. The stiff, trailing branches hang neatly from the sides of pots and baskets or spread politely over the ground, filling in and knitting together perennials, annuals and even shrubs. This irreplaceable plant will likely be a favorite in your garden every summer.

PLANTING

Seeding: Not recommended.

Planting out: After last frost.

Spacing: About 30" (75 cm).

GROWING

Licorice plant prefers **full sun**. The soil should be of **poor to average fertility**, neutral or alkaline and **well drained**. Plant will wilt if the soil dries out but revives quickly once watered.

Include this plant in your hanging baskets and container plantings, and the trailing growth will quickly fill in, providing a soft silvery backdrop for the colorful flowers. Licorice plant can also be used in beds and borders as an edger or an annual groundcover. In rock gardens and along the tops of retaining walls, licorice plant will cascade down over the rocks in a silvery wave.

This plant is grown for the foliage, not the flowers and is a perennial that is grown as an annual.

'Silver'

RECOMMENDED

'Limelight' has bright lime green leaves that need protection from direct sunlight to maintain their color. It is less common, though well worth hunting for (photo on opposite page).

'Silver' is a common cultivar. The gray-green leaves are covered in a silvery white down.

'Variegatum' has gray-green leaves that are dappled or margined in a silvery shade of cream. It is also a less-common cultivar.

GARDENING TIPS

This plant is a good indicator plant for hanging baskets. When you see this plant wilting, it is time to get out the hose or watering can.

It is easy to start more plants from cuttings in fall. Then you will have a supply of new plants for the following spring. Once they have rooted, keep the young plants in a cool, bright room for winter.

PROBLEMS & PESTS

Powdery mildew can be an occasional problem, though you might not see it, because the leaves are already soft and white.

Livingstone Daisy
Ice Plant
Dorotheanthus bellidiformis
(formerly called *Mesembryanthemum criniflorum*)

Flower color: Crimson, orange, rose, yellow, pink, white or bicolored.
Height: 6" (15 cm). **Spread:** 12" (30 cm).

*T*he silvery leaves on this low-growing plant appear to be covered with ice that is ready to melt against the hot, bright colors of the daisy-like blooms. If you have a seaside garden, you will enjoy this annual planted between boulders and flat rocks. It can form a carpet of color to contrast with ornamental grasses and nasturtium, which are two annual flowers that also thrive in a sandy, seaside soil.

PLANTING

Seeding: Indoors in late winter; direct sow in spring.

Planting out: After last frost.

Spacing: 12" (30 cm).

GROWING

Livingstone daisy likes to grow in **full sun**. The soil should be **sandy** and **well drained,** with **poor to average fertility**. Brightly flowered, low-growing plants can be used for edging in borders, on dry slopes, in rock gardens or in mixed containers. They can also be used between the stones or around the edges of a paved patio.

RECOMMENDED

Harlequin Mixed is a bright color mix, with white or yellow shading around the eye.

Magic Carpet Series comes in a variety of colors.

PROBLEMS & PESTS

Slugs, snails and aphids may be troublesome.

These plants are also known as 'ice plants' because of the tiny crystals that form on the leaves.

The flowers close on cloudy days.

Lobelia
Edging Lobelia
Lobelia erinus

Flower color: Purple, blue, pink, white or red.
Height: 3–9" (8–23 cm). **Spread:** 6" (15 cm) or wider.

*T*he first flower I ever grew from seed was lobelia, and the dust-like seed specks are surprisingly easy to grow. I planted the deep blue 'Crystal Palace' lobelia in small clay pots, and set them in a row alongside a path in my first garden. From this experience, I learned that lobelia needs a lot of water and is one of the loveliest plants for adding color to shady spots. Its delicate beauty blends well with dangling fuchsias and cascading begonias. Luckily, lobelia also does well in the sun because sky blue lobelias and sunshine yellow marigolds are the blue-and-yellow duo voted most memorable by garden club members.

PLANTING

Seeding: Indoors in mid-winter.

Planting out: After last frost.

Spacing: 6" (15 cm).

GROWING

Lobelia grows well in **full sun** or **partial shade**. The soil should be **fertile, high in organic matter, moist** and **fairly well drained**. Lobelia likes cool summer nights.

Because seedlings are prone to damping off, be sure to use good, clean seed-starting soil mix. Damping off causes plants to rot at soil level, flop over and die.

These plants are popular for use along the edges of beds and borders, in rock gardens or rock walls or in mixed containers or hanging baskets.

RECOMMENDED

Cascade Series is a trailing form that comes in blue, lilac, white or pink.

'Crystal Palace' is a compact plant that rarely achieves 4" (10 cm) in height. This cultivar has dark green foliage and dark blue flowers.

'Sapphire' has blue flowers and a white eye, and it is good for trailing from hanging baskets and window boxes.

GARDENING TIPS

Trim lobelia back once the first wave of flowers has passed. This step will keep the plant flowering throughout summer. In hot areas, this plant may die back over summer, but they usually bounce back as the weather cools.

PROBLEMS & PESTS

Rust, leaf spot and slugs may be troublesome.

'Sapphire'

Cascade Series

Love-in-a-Mist
Devil-in-a-Bush
Nigella damascena

Flower color: Blue, white, pink or purple.
Height: 12–30" (30–75 cm). **Spread:** 8–12" (20–30 cm).

Such a romantic name fits this fragile-looking flower. The delicate, fern-like foliage is the mist, and the pink, white or blue blooms represents love. Old fashioned and charming, use *Nigella* in the cutting garden or in the front or middle of the border. The flowers will fade and disappear as summer progresses, but interesting seedpods and a habit of reseeding makes up for the short lifespan. Pair this early summer bloomer with pansies and violas, or use it for a wildflower look blooming beside an old plow or alongside a rustic split-rail fence.

One summer, love-in-a-mist bloomed for me inside an old metal coal scuttle, and the look was that of an abandoned garden, flowering freely as the foliage swayed in the gentlest breeze.

Nigella is difficult to transplant, and direct sowing is recommended.

PLANTING

Seeding: Indoors in peat pots or pellets in late winter; direct sow in early spring.

Planting out: Mid-spring.

Spacing: 10–15" (25–38 cm).

GROWING

Love-in-a-mist prefers to grow in **full sun**. Soil should be of **average fertility** and **light and well drained**. Attractive, airy plants are often used in mixed beds and borders where the flowers appear to be floating over the delicate foliage. The blooming may slow down and the plants may die back if the weather gets too hot for them during summer.

These plants resent having their roots disturbed. Plants started indoors should be in peat pots or pellets to avoid damaging the roots when the plant is transplanted into the garden. Seeds can be started directly in the garden in fall. Be sure to provide the young plants with protection over winter. Sow seeds at two week intervals all spring to prolong the blooming period.

RECOMMENDED

Miss Jekyll Series are semi-double cultivars in rose pink, sky blue or deep cornflower blue that pairs especially well with golden yellow coreopsis in a rich duet of royal blue and regal gold. The plants grow to about 18" (45 cm) in height.

Persian Jewel Series is one of the most common cultivars with flowers in all colors. They usually grow to 15" (38 cm) tall.

GARDENING TIPS

The stems of this plant can be a bit floppy and may benefit from being staked with twiggy branches. Poke the branches in around the plants while they are young and the plants will grow up between the twigs.

Love-in-a-mist has a tendency to self-sow and may show up in unexpected spots in your garden for years to come.

Both the flowers and the seedpods are popular for flower arrangements. The flowers are long lasting in fresh arrangements and the pods can be dried once they are ripe and used in dried arrangements.

Madagascar Periwinkle

Catharanthus roseus

Flower color: Red, rose, pink, mauve or white; often with contrasting centers.
Height: 6–24" (15–60 cm). **Spread:** Usually equal to or greater than height.

It takes an extra hot summer to get this tender plant to bloom in cool coastal gardens but farther inland, where summers are warmer, this periwinkle will open its creamy white or pink-centered blooms. The compact form of Madagascar periwinkle makes it a tidy companion plant in flowerbeds. Pair periwinkle with early bloomers such as forget-me-not or pansies—the late summer blooms will take over when the early bloomers fade away in mid-summer. Planting mums and *Sedum* 'Autumn Joy' nearby will create quite a show of blooms in the fall garden.

PLANTING

Seeding: Indoors in mid-winter.

Planting out: After last frost.

Spacing: 8–18" (20–45 cm).

GROWING

Madagascar periwinkle prefers **full sun** but tolerates partial shade. Any soil is fine. These plants will tolerate pollution and drought but prefer to be watered regularly, and they don't like to be too wet or too cold.

Keep seedlings warm and take care not to overwater them. The soil temperature should be 55–64° F (13–18° C) for seeds to germinate.

Madagascar periwinkle will do well in the sunny, warmest part of the garden. Plant in a bed along an exposed driveway or against the south-facing wall of the house. These periwinkles can also be used in hanging baskets, planters and as temporary groundcovers.

RECOMMENDED

Pacifica Series has a variety of flower colors on compact plants.

GARDENING TIPS

This plant is a perennial that is grown as an annual. In a bright room, it can be grown as a houseplant.

PROBLEMS & PESTS

Slugs can be troublesome. Most rot and fungus-related problems can be avoided by not overwatering the plants.

One of the best annuals to use in front of homes or busy streets. Madagascar periwinkle will bloom happily despite exposure to exhaust fumes, dust and lack of water.

Mallow

Lavatera trimestris

Flower color: Rose, pink, salmon or white.
Height: 24–48" (60–120 cm). **Spread:** 18–24" (45–60 cm).

*T*he simple, cup-shaped flowers that grow from fat, pointed buds have delicate, red-veined petals the thickness of fine tissue paper. It's hard to believe such soft and delicate blooms can thrive in such tough growing conditions. I grow mallow in front of a cedar hedge, where the gray leaves stand out against the deep green of the cedar. Many flowers have failed in the dry, infertile soil near this evergreen hedge, but mallow is mellow and just keeps blooming, stopping only when the first hard frost of fall announces the start of winter.

PLANTING

Seeding: Indoors in late winter; direct sow in spring.

Planting out: After last frost.

Spacing: 18–24" (45–60 cm).

'Mont Blanc'

GROWING

Mallow prefers **full sun**. The soil should be of **average fertility, light** and **well drained**. This plant likes cool, moist weather. Select a protected site because it doesn't like to be exposed to too much wind. These plants resent having their roots disturbed when they are transplanted and tend to do better when planted directly in the garden. If you choose to start seeds indoors, a good approach is to use peat pots.

These plants grow to be fairly large and shrubby. They can be used in a variety of ways. In a bed or border they can be used behind smaller plants to provide a colorful backdrop. Along a property line or driveway, they can be used as temporary hedges. The flowers can be used for cutting and are edible.

Though there are only 25 species of Lavatera, they are a diverse group containing annuals, biennials, perennials and shrubs.

L. cachemiriana

RECOMMENDED

Beauty Series are available in a variety of colors.

'Mont Blanc' bears white flowers on a compact plant that grows to about 20" (50 cm) tall.

'Silver Cup' has cup-shaped, light pink flowers, with dark pink veins.

ALTERNATE SPECIES

L. arborea (tree mallow) is a large plant, capable of growing to 10' (3 m) tall and spreading 5' (1.5 m). The funnel-shaped flowers are pinkish purple in color. The lifespan of this plant is undetermined; typically grown as an annual, it can sometimes be treated as a biennial or perennial. The cultivar **'Variegata'** has cream-colored mottling on its leaves.

L. cachemiriana has light pink flowers. It can grow up to 8' (2.5 m) tall and is usually half as wide. It is native to Kashmir.

'Silver Cup'

GARDENING TIPS

Stake tall varieties to keep them from falling over in summer rain.

PROBLEMS & PESTS

Plant in well-drained soil to avoid root rot. Destroy any rust-infected plants.

Tree mallow is a good choice for seaside gardens because it is tolerant of coastal conditions.

Marigold

Tagetes spp.

Flower color: Yellow, red, orange or cream and bicolors.
Height: 6–36" (15–90 cm) tall, depending on species and variety.
Spread: 12–18" (30–45 cm).

Nothing says summer like the bright yellow blooms of marigolds. The sunshine colors on this sun-loving plant are perfect for using in a Victorian-inspired sun garden. Plant orange, yellow and gold marigolds in the shape of the sun, with the taller types in a center circle and the lower varieties radiating outwards. You can use a shovel to dig out sod from your lawn to form the outline of the sunshine garden, much like the Victorians did for their intricate bedding displays. Marigolds are an easy-to-grow flower.

PLANTING

Seeding: Spring or earlier if starting indoors.

Planting out: Once soil has warmed.

Spacing: Dwarf marigolds, 6" (15 cm); tall marigolds, 12" (30 cm).

T. erecta

GROWING

Marigolds grow best in **full sun**. The soil should be of **average fertility** and **well drained**. These plants are drought-tolerant.

Mass-planted or mixed with other plants, marigolds make a vibrant addition to beds, borders and container gardens.

To use as cut flowers, remove lower leaves to cut back on the pungent scent.

T. patula

T. tenuifolia is used as a culinary or tea herb in some Latin American countries.

RECOMMENDED

T. erecta (African marigold; American marigold; Aztec marigold) is 20–36" (50–90 cm) tall, with huge flowers. **'Marvel'** is a more compact cultivar growing only 18" (45 cm) tall, but with the large flowers that made this species popular.

T. patula (French marigold) is low-growing and 7–10" (18–25 cm) tall. **Bonanza Series** is another popular double-flowered cultivar. Flowers are in red, orange, yellow and bicolors. **Janie Series** is a popular double-flowered cultivar, with red, orange and yellow blooms. It is early blooming and the plants are compact.

T. tenuifolia (signet marigold) has dainty, single flowers that grow on bushy plants with feathery foliage. **Gem Series** is commonly available with flowers in shades of yellow and orange; and the blooms last all summer. The compact plants grow about 10" (25 cm) tall.

T. tenuifolia

GARDENING TIPS

Remove spent blooms to encourage more flowers and to keep plants tidy.

These plants will thrive in the hottest, driest parts of your garden.

PROBLEMS & PESTS

Slugs and snails can eat seedlings to the ground.

T. erecta *and* T. patula *are often used in vegetable gardens for their reputed insect-repelling abilities.*

T. patula

Mexican Sunflower

Tithonia rotundifolia

Flower color: Orange, red-orange or yellow-orange.
Height: 4–6' (1.2–1.8 m). **Spread:** 12–24" (30–60 cm).

*T*he warmth, excitement and vibrant colors of a fiesta give the Mexican sunflower its common name. Bright and feisty, these flowers happily gather together against the sunny side of a wall or blossom from clay pots on a sunny patio. Their sombrero-like blooms entice butterflies to visit.

PLANTING

Seeding: Indoors in early spring;
direct sow in spring.

Planting out: Once soil has warmed.

Spacing: 12–24" (30–60 cm).

GROWING

Mexican sunflowers grow best in **full sun**. The
soil should be of **average to poor fertility** and
well drained. Because these plants are heat-
resistant, they are ideal for growing in a sunny,
dry, warm spot in the garden—under the eaves of
a south-facing wall is one good spot. They are tall
and break easily if exposed to too much wind.
A wall or fence will provide some shelter and
stability. These annuals are coarse in appearance
and are well suited to the back of a border where
they can provide a good backdrop to a bed of
shorter annuals.

Cover seeds lightly because they germinate more
evenly and quickly when exposed to some light.

RECOMMENDED

'**Torch**' has bright red-orange flowers.

'**Yellow Torch**' has bright yellow flowers.

GARDENING TIPS

Your Mexican sunflower needs little water or care,
however, it will bloom more prolifically if it is
deadheaded regularly.

PROBLEMS & PESTS

This plant is generally resistant to most problems,
however, young foliage may suffer slug and snail
damage. Aphids can become a real pest if not
dealt with immediately.

*For a hot look along a sunny fence or wall mix
Mexican sunflowers with common sunflowers
and marigolds.*

*Sear ends of cut flowers
with a flame.*

'Torch'

Million Bells

Calibrachoa

Calibrachoa Hybrids

Flower color: Pink, purple, yellow, orange or white.
Height: 6–12" (15 cm). **Spread:** Up to 24" (60 cm).

A floriferous newcomer to the annual selection, these heavy bloomers look like miniature petunias, with graceful, bell-shaped blossoms, and their trailing habit makes them perfect for window boxes, baskets and for use as groundcovers. Their best feature is their long blooming habit. You can buy a basket of million bells in May and it will bloom well into fall as the flowers develop a hardiness as the weather cools and can survive temperatures down to the 20° F (-7° C).

PLANTING

Seeding: May not be available.

Planting out: After last frost.

Spacing: 6–15" (15–38 cm).

GROWING

Million bells prefer to grow in **full sun**. Soil should be **fertile, moist** and **well drained**. Preferring to be watered regularly, they are fairly drought resistant in cool and warm climates.

Popular plants for planters and hanging baskets, they are also attractive in beds and borders where their trailing habit will blend them between other plants. These plants grow all summer and need plenty of room to spread or they will overtake other flowers. In a hanging basket they will toll out millions of bell-shaped blooms.

RECOMMENDED

Calibrachoa hybrids are a new and distinct species developed from petunias.

The **Million Bells Series** includes **'Trailing Pink'** with rose-pink, yellow-centered flowers, **'Trailing Blue'** (photo on opposite page) with dark blue or purple, yellow-centered flowers and **'Trailing White'** with white, yellow-centered flowers. **'Terracotta'** with reddish orange flowers and **'Yellow'** with bright yellow flowers, truly distinguish million bells from petunias.

GARDENING TIPS

Pinch back to keep plants compact.

To protect the petals from damaging rain, place hanging baskets under the eaves of the house or porch.

PROBLEMS & PESTS

Wet weather and cloudy days could cause leaf spots and delayed blooming. Watch for slugs and earwigs that like to nibble on the petals.

'Trailing Pink'

'Trailing Pink' and 'Trailing Blue'

Morning Glory

Ipomea tricolor

Flower color: White, blue, pink or purple and variegated.
Height: 10–12' (3–3.5 m). **Spread:** 12–24" (30–60 cm).

Morning glory is the day-shift cousin to moonflower, opening in heavenly shades of blue or rose pink with the rise of the sun. It will embellish a cyclone fence, a wire topiary structure or any object thin enough to twine its tendrils around. The most imaginative use I've seen with these vines was in a wire basket secured to the handlebars of an old bike. The basket was lined with moss and filled with a mixture of annuals. The petunias and geraniums provided the bulk of color, but it was the morning glory that caught everyone's attention. Spilling from the basket, it twined itself all around the frame of the bike, working tendrils through the spokes of the wheels and spiraling over the handlebars. Once established, stand back and watch out, because this vine grows fast.

PLANTING

Seeding: Indoors in early spring; direct sow after last frost.

Planting out: Late spring.

Spacing: 12–18" (30–45 cm).

GROWING

Grow *Ipomea* in **full sun**. Any type of soil will do, but a **light, well-drained** soil of **poor fertility** is preferred. Soak seeds for 24 hours before sowing. Sow in individual peat pots if choosing to start them indoors.

Morning glory can be grown anywhere: fences, walls, trees, trellises and arbours are all possible frames for morning glories. As a ground-cover, it will grow along the ground and over any obstacles it encounters. It can also be grown in hanging baskets.

Each flower of morning glory lasts for only one day. The buds form a spiral that slowly unfurls as the day brightens with the rising sun.

RECOMMENDED

There are several cultivars, including the popular **'Heavenly Blue,'** which has true sky blue flowers, with a white centre.

I. tricolor

I. alba

ALTERNATE SPECIES

I. alba (moonflower) has sweet-scented, white flowers that only open at night. It grows up to 15' (4.5 m) tall.

I. batatas (sweet potato vine) is a twining climber that is grown for its foliage rather than its flowers. Often used in planters and hanging baskets, sweet potato vine can be used by itself or mixed with other plants. Initially developed for the tubers or sweet potatoes that form on the roots this plant has recieved a recent increase in popularity when grown for its attractive foliage. **'Blackie'** has dark purple, almost black, deeply lobed leaves. **'Terrace Lime'** has yellow green foliage on a fairly compact plant. These cascading plants can also be trained to grow up a trellis. As an added bonus, when you pull up your plants at the end of the summer you can eat the tubers (sweet potatoes).

'Blackie'

Moonflowers are sweetly scented and open only at night and sometimes on cloudy days. Grow them on a porch or on a trellis near a patio that is used in the evenings, so the flowers can be fully enjoyed. They need warm weather to bloom. The buds may close on cloudy days, but once evening falls, the huge, white blossoms pour forth their sweet nectar, attracting exotic night-flying moths.

GARDENING TIPS

Morning glories must twine around objects in order to climb them. Wide fence posts, walls or other broad objects too large to twine around must have a trellis or some wire or twine attached to them to provide the vines with something to grow up.

If you have a bright sunny window, consider starting a hanging basket of morning glories indoors for a unique winter display. The vines will twine around the hangers and spill over the sides of the pot, providing you with beautiful trumpet flowers, regardless of the weather outside.

PROBLEMS & PESTS

Morning glory is susceptible to several fungal problems, but they occur only rarely.

Sweet potato vine is best recognized by the large lime green, heart-shaped leaves, but it is also available in shades of purple. Unlike the more aggressive members of the family, sweet potato vines don't twine or grasp or get carried away. They drape politely over the sides of containers or spread neatly over the soil beneath taller plants.

'Terrace Lime'

Nasturtium

Tropaeolum majus

Flower color: Red, orange, yellow, pink, white or bicolored.
Height: 12–18" (30–45 cm) for dwarf varieties; up to 10' (3 m) for trailing varieties.
Spread: Equal to or a bit wider than height.

A brick planter box in the hot sun is a perfect spot for nasturtiums, and their round leaves are a lovely contrast to the geometric angles of the brickwork. If you have a rock wall near the patio, be sure have some nasturtiums draping over the boulders. On barbecuing nights, you can conveniently pluck a peppery nasturtium bloom to garnish your hamburger in place of a pickle, or you can use the blossoms to spice up a summer salad. Naturtiums are also great beach-house guests, often reseeding themselves year after year if the winter is mild and rarely complaining if you forget to water them on a sunny day.

PLANTING

Seeding: Indoors in late winter; direct sow in mid-spring.

Planting out: After last frost.

Spacing: 12" (30 cm).

GROWING

Nasturtiums prefer **full sun** but will tolerate partial shade. The soil should be of **average to poor fertility, light, moist** and **well drained**. Let the soil drain completely between waterings.

If you start nasturtium seeds indoors, sow them in individual peat pots.

Nasturtiums are used in beds, borders, containers, hanging baskets and on sloped banks. The climbing varieties are also used to grow up trellises or over rocks in walls and other places that need concealing.

These plants thrive in poor locations and a they make an interesting addition to plantings made on hard to mow slopes where many other plants are difficult to grow.

Jewel Series

RECIPE
POOR MAN'S CAPERS (PICKLED NASTURTIUM SEEDS)

Soak green seeds in a brine made from 2 cups (250 ml) of water and 1 tsp. (12 ml) of salt for 24 hours.

Fill small sterilized jars with the seeds, a peeled clove of garlic and 1 tsp. (12 ml) of pickling spices.

Heat white wine vinegar to the simmering point and fill each jar.

Seal with acid-proof lids and let the seeds sit for about a month.

The seeds should be eaten within a week after opening.

Nasturtiums have a place in the vegetable or herb garden. The leaves and flowers are edible and can be added to salads, soups and dips to add a peppery flavor. The unripe seeds are pickled and used as a replacement for capers.

Some gardeners believe that these annuals attract and harbor certain pests, like whitefly and aphids, and that nasturtiums should not be grown near plants that are susceptible to the same problems. Other gardeners believe that these plants are preferred by pest insects and that the pests will flock to them and leave the rest of the garden alone. Still other gardeners claim that these plants, because of the high sulfur levels in the leaves, repel many pests that would otherwise infest the garden. I have yet to notice an influence, for the better or the worse, on the pest populations in my garden.

RECOMMENDED

Nasturtiums have been greatly improved by hybridizing. The foliage of the older varieties tended to hide the flowers. New varieties hold their flowers (available in a great selection of colors) above the foliage. There are also some new and interesting cultivars with variegated foliage and compact, attractive, mound-forming habits.

Alaska Series has green-and-white marbled foliage.

Double Dwarf Jewel Series has compact plants that grow to 12" (30 cm) tall and wide, with double flowers.

Jewel Series has a mix of deep orange, red and gold blooms.

'Peach Melba' forms a 12" (30 cm) mound. The flowers are pale yellow with a bright orange and red splash at the base of each petal.

PROBLEMS & PESTS

The few problems that afflict nasturtiums include aphids, slugs, whiteflies and some viruses.

Alaska Series

Nicotiana
Flowering Tobacco Plant
Nicotiana alata

Flower color: Red, pink, green, yellow, white or purple.
Height: Up to 5' (1.5 m); 12–18" (30–45 cm) for dwarf varieties.
Spread: 12" (30 cm).

*T*his annual flower has sticky foliage, much like its cousin the petunia, but nicotiana has an advantage over the petunia: the spent flowers fall free from the plant, eliminating the need for deadheading. The tall, elegant blooms remind me of swans with their long necks, and they make great companions for lower-growing plantings of petunias. You can add the attractive scent of nicotiana to a patio by using its vertical form in the center of a container display.

PLANTING
Seeding: Indoors in early spring; direct sow later.

Planting out: Once soil has warmed.

Spacing: 8–12" (20–30 cm).

GROWING

Nicotiana will grow equally well in **full sun** or **light or partial shade**. The soil should be **fertile, high in organic matter, moist** and **well drained**.

The seeds require light for germination, so leave them uncovered.

These plants are popular in beds and borders. The dwarf varieties do well in containers.

RECOMMENDED

'Grandiflora' grows 24" (60 cm) tall and has a strong, sweet fragrance.

Nicki Series has many colored, fragrant blooms that open all day. The compact plants grow up to 18" (45 cm) tall.

Nicki Series

N. sylvestris (top)
Nicki Series (bottom)

ALTERNATE SPECIES

***N. sylvestris* 'Fragrant Cloud'** has white blooms that give off a scent in the evening, and it grows up to 4' (1.2 m) tall.

GARDENING TIPS

Do not plant nicotiana near tomatoes because they are members of the same plant family and share many of the same diseases. The tobacco may attract and harbor diseases that can kill tomatoes but hardly affect nicotiana.

PROBLEMS & PESTS

Tobacco mosaic virus, aphids and downy or powdery mildew may cause occasional problems.

*Like sweet peas, nicotiana was originally cultivated for the wonderful scent of the flowers. At first, the flowers were only available in a greenish color and they only opened in the evening and at night.
In attempts to expand the variety of colors and have the flowers open during the day, the popular scent has, in some cases, been lost.*

Painted-Tongue
Velvet Flower
Salpiglossis sinuata

Flower color: Red, yellow, orange, pink, purple; often patterned bicolors.
Height: Up to about 24" (60 cm). **Spread:** 12" (30 cm).

Grow this petunia-like annual for its red, orange, rust and bicolored blooms that look like they have been dipped in an amber antique stain. The rich tones give even new gardens the satisfying hue of an established landscape. Paired with the warm rusty tones of fall mums in a terra cotta pot or used against the gray patina of aged wood in a barn or fence, these colors are mellow and calming. I remember photographers flocked to a show garden one summer when this unusual annual was paired with the low-growing, peach-colored alyssum and planted in an antique and rusted wheelbarrow. Any old or rusty novelty container will complement the rich patina of the painted-tongue blooms.

PLANTING

Seeding: Indoors in late winter; direct sow in spring.

Planting out: After last frost.

Spacing: 12" (30 cm).

GROWING

Painted-tongue prefers **full sun**. The soil should be **fertile, rich in organic matter** and **well drained**.

Seeds are very tiny and shouldn't be covered with soil. Seeds will germinate more evenly if kept in darkness until they sprout—cover pots with dark plastic, layers of newspaper or by placing pots in a dark closet. Once they start to sprout, they can be moved into light.

Like petunias, these flowers can become battered in rainy and windy conditions. Plant them in warm, sheltered areas of the garden. Painted-tongue is useful in the middle or back of beds and borders. They can also be used in large mixed containers.

RECOMMENDED

'Blue Peacock' has blue flowers with yellow throats and dark veins.

Casino Series are early blooming and tolerant of rain and wind. Flowers are in a wide range of colors.

PROBLEMS & PESTS

Occasional problems with aphids or root rot are possible.

The irridescent quality of these flowers causes their color to change as they turn in a breeze.

'Blue Peacock'

Petunia

Petunia x *hybrida*

Flower color: Pink. purple, red, white, yellow or bicolored.
Height: 6–18" (15–45 cm). **Spread:** 12–24" (30–60 cm) or wider.

*T*here are three basic groups of petunias. The grandifloras have the largest flowers—up to 4" (10 cm) across. The widest variety of colors and forms are available in the grandifloras, but they are the most likely to be damaged by heavy rain. The multifloras have smaller flowers, about half the size of the grandifloras, but bear many more flowers. They are more tolerant of adverse weather conditions. The millifloras are the newest group. Like petunias in miniature, these flowers are about 1" (2.5 cm) across and are borne profusely over the whole plant. They are extremely tolerant of wet weather conditions, sometimes even self-seeding. When considering where to plant, remember that petunias are 'pillow bloomers,' filling in and fluffing out in large blocks or drifts of color.

PLANTING

Seeding: Indoors in mid-winter.

Planting out: After last frost.

Spacing: 12–18" (30–45 cm).

GROWING

Petunias prefer **full sun**. The soil should be of **poor to average fertility, sandy** and **well drained**. Use petunias in beds, borders, containers and hanging baskets. When sowing, press seeds into soil surface but don't cover with soil.

For speedy growth, prolific blooming and ease of care, petunias are hard to beat. Even the most neglected plants will continue to bloom all summer. The huge selection of plant habits, flower colors and sizes ensures that there is a petunia for every garden.

Multiflora Variety

Multiflora variety

RECOMMENDED

Carpet Series is a multiflora variety, available in a wide variety of colors.

Daddy Series is a grandiflora variety, available in darkly veined shades of pink and purple.

Fantasty Series is a milliflora variety, available in shades of red, purple, pink and white, although the pinks tend to be the easiest to find. With this series' growing popularity, more colors will likely become available. These petunias are popular in mixed containers and hanging baskets and are also very nice in garden beds, forming neat mounds of foliage and flowers.

Supercascade Series is a grandiflora variety, available in a wide variety of colors.

Ultra Series is a grandiflora variety, available in many colors, including bicolors. This variety of grandiflora recovers quite quickly from weather damage.

Wave Series is a multiflora variety, available in pink and purple. It recovers well from rain damage, blooms a lot and spreads quickly. It is a popular variety for hanging baskets and containers.

Grandiflora variety

GARDENING TIPS

Pinch halfway back in midsummer to keep plants bushy and encourage new growth and flowers.

PROBLEMS & PESTS

Aphids and fungus may be problems. The fungus problems can be avoided by not wetting the foliage, if possible, and by providing a location with good drainage.

Multiflora variety

Grandiflora variety

Milliflora variety

Phlox
Phlox drummondii

Flower color: Purple, pink, red, blue, white or yellow.
Height: 6–18" (15–45 cm). **Spread:** 10" (25 cm) or wider.

*T*o say the color on a blooming phlox is intense is an understatement. The blooms are so saturated with color that when driving past a country cottage I slowed down just to appreciate the phlox border blooming alongside the fence. This annual is for large gardens or long borders because you can easily multiply these flowers by taking stem cuttings and poking them into soft soil. Pair these bright bloomers between the intense colors of delphiniums and low-growing midnight blue lobelia or bright yellow dwarf marigolds and enjoy a garden of animated technicolor blooms.

PLANTING

Seeding: Direct sow in early spring.

Spacing: Up to 8" (20 cm).

GROWING

Phlox prefers **full sun**. The soil should be **fertile, moist** and **well drained**. Use phlox in beds, borders, containers, rock gardens, rock walls and coastal gardens.

These plants resent being transplanted and starting them indoors is not recommended. Germination takes 10–15 days. These plants can be spaced quite close together.

RECOMMENDED

Palona Series is a compact, heavy-blooming plant that grows 8–10" (20–25 cm) tall. Flowers come in many colors, often with contrasting centers.

Twinkle Mixed has unusual, small, star-shaped flowers on compact plants, 8" (20 cm) tall. The petal margins and centers often contrast with the main petal color.

GARDENING TIPS

Deadhead to promote blooming.

Plant cuttings in moist soil and they will easily root.

To discourage disease, do not over-water or let the foliage stay wet at night.

PROBLEMS & PESTS

There are fungal problems that can develop in phlox, but they can, for the most part, be avoided by providing good drainage and avoiding having water standing on the leaves late in the day. Water them in the morning during dry spells and avoid handling wet foliage.

Poppy

Shirley Poppy

Papaver rhoeas

Flower color: Red, pink, white, purple, yellow or orange.
Height: 24–36" (60–90 cm). **Spread:** 12" (30 cm).

Celebrate early summer with the silky, translucent petals and enthusiastic blooms of the poppy, also known as corn poppy or flanders poppy. It is the perfect transitional flower to use for masses of color between the spring bulb season and the perennials and annuals that bloom in high summer. The best display of poppies I've ever seen was a colony that escaped the flowerbed and reseeded itself in a gravel pathway. It grew thicker over the years as mother plants dropped seeds before fading away in the summer heat. The poppy is also a very patriotic flower; the deep red 'Legion of Honor' variety has significant symbolism to World War II veterans, who saw it blooming through the open fields of Western Europe.

PLANTING

Seeding: Direct sow every two weeks starting in early spring.

Spacing: 12" (30 cm).

GROWING

Poppies grow best in **full sun**. The soil should be **fertile, sandy** and have **lots of organic matter** mixed in. Good drainage is essential. Do not start seeds indoors because transplanting is often unsuccessful.

Poppies are good for use in mixed borders where plants are slow to fill in. Poppies will fill in empty spaces early in the season, then the foliage dies back over summer, leaving room for the other plants. They can also be used in rock gardens and the cut flowers are popular for fresh arrangements. Deadhead to prolong blooms.

The seeds of both Shirley poppy and opium poppy can be used to flavor baked goods like muffins, breads and bagels.

RECOMMENDED

'Champagne Bubbles' is a strong, bushy plant, with lots of pastel flowers.

Shirley Series has silky, cup-shaped petals. Flowers come in many colors and can be single, semi-double or double.

ALTERNATE SPECIES

P. somniferum (opium poppy) grows up to 48" (120 cm) tall. The flowers are red, pink, white or purple. This plant has a mixed reputation. It is the source of several drugs, including codeine, morphine and opium. All parts of the plant can cause stomach upset except for the seeds, which are a popular culinary additive (poppy seeds). The seeds contain none of the chemicals that make this plant pharmaceutically valuable. The large seed capsules are also dried and used in floral arrangements. Though propagation of the species is restricted in many countries there are several attractive cultivars that have been developed for ornamental use. 'Peony Flowered' has large frilly double flowers in a variety of colors on plants that grow up to 36" (90 cm) tall. 'Danebrog Lace' is an old cultivar originating in the nineteenth century. The single flowers have frilly red petals with a large white patch at the base of each petal.

P. somniferum 'Peony Flowered'

GARDENING TIPS

Mix tiny seeds with sand for even sowing.

Be careful when weeding around faded summer plants; you may accidentally pull up late summer poppy seedlings.

PROBLEMS & PESTS

Poppies rarely have problems, although fungus can occur if the soil is wet and poorly drained.

For cut flowers, stick the cut end of stem in a flame or boiling water to seal them.

Portulaca
Moss Rose
Portulaca grandiflora

Flower color: Red, pink, yellow, white, purple or orange.
Height: 4–8" (10–20 cm). **Spread:** 6–12" (15–30 cm) or wider.

*F*orgetful gardeners will love this annual, also known as rose moss, because it blooms continuously even if left unwatered. In a hanging basket on a sunny porch or trailing through a rockery with dry, sandy soil, the rose-like papery blooms will spill forth in brilliant color despite the summer heat. Portulaca makes a great display in a parking strip paired up with gazania, strawflowers, boulders and gravel for a drought- and heat-resistant display. The thin but succulent leaves make an interesting textural contrast against the white-washed or stucco walls of Spanish- inspired architecture.

PLANTING

Seeding: Indoors in late winter.

Planting out: Once soil has warmed.

Spacing: 12" (30 cm).

GROWING

Portulaca requires **full sun**. The soil should be of **poor fertility, sandy** and **well drained**. To ensure that you will have plants where you want them, seed indoors. If you seed outdoors after the last frost date, tiny seeds may get washed away in rainstorms and the plants won't be where you want them.

Close spacing isn't a problem and causes plants to intermingle, resulting in well-mixed flower colors. Portulaca is the ideal plant for garden spots that just don't get enough water, under the eaves of the house or in dry, rocky, exposed areas. These plants are ideal for people who like having backets hanging from the front porch but always forget to water. As long as the location is sunny, the plants will do well, with minimal care.

RECOMMENDED

'**Afternoon Delight**' has flowers that stay open in the evening.

Sundial Series has been developed to perform well in cooler, cloudier climates. It has double flowers.

'**Wildfire**' has single flowers and is good for placing in hanging baskets.

PROBLEMS & PESTS

If portulaca has excellent drainage and as much light as possible, it shouldn't have problems.

These plants will fill a sunny, exposed, narrow strip of soil, between any paving and the foundation of a house, with bright colors all summer. They require only minimal attention.

Prairie Gentian
Lisianthius
Eustoma grandiflora

Flower color: Blue, purple, pink, yellow or white.
Height: 6–24" (15–60 cm). **Spread:** Usually half the height.

This cup-shaped bloomer will add a decidedly alpine look to sunny garden beds. The true blue variety is a knock out when paired with bright yellow marigolds or other sunny yellow, heat-loving flowers, and the purple and pinks can be grown in front of taller, white shasta daisies for beautiful contrasts in form and color. Children enjoy popping the thumb-sized buds.

PLANTING

Seeding: Indoors in early winter.

Planting out: Mid-spring.

Spacing: 4–12" (10–30 cm), depending on expected mature size of variety.

GROWING

Prairie gentian prefers **full sun** but will tolerate light or partial shade. The soil should be of **average fertility** and **well drained**. A neutral or alkaline pH is preferred. If your soil is very acidic, then grow the dwarf varieties in pots with an appropriate growing mix, instead of struggling to keep these plants healthy in the garden beds. If planting directly in the garden, remember that seedlings can be quite slow to establish.

The tallest varieties are very popular in cut flower gardens as they have very long-lasting blooms. All varieties of plants are best when grouped in flowerbeds or containers.

RECOMMENDED

Echo Series also comes in many colors. This popular tall variety is admired for its double flowers that are excellent for cutflower arrangements. It grows to about 24" (60 cm) tall.

Lisa Series comes in many colors and is a popular dwarf variety. This series is also reputed to bloom from seed one month sooner than other varieties. This plant grows to about 8" (20 cm) tall.

PROBLEMS & PESTS

Generally, this plant is trouble free, however, several diseases can kill prairie gentian. Fusarium wilt is one of them. Purchase treated seed from reputable sources and destroy any plants that appear to be diseased before the diseases have a chance to spread to other plants.

A small vase filled with satin-textured prairie gentian flowers will asdd a touch of elegance to any table.

Prickly Poppy

Argemone mexicana

Flower color: White, yellow or lavender.
Height: 36–60" (90–150 cm). **Spread:** 12–24" (30–60 cm).

A real conversation plant and one sure to make the neighbors sit up and pay attention, especially if used along the property line to keep wandering dogs and children from taking shortcuts. The drought-resistant nature of this desert plant makes it a good companion for sedums, succulents and other plants with gray or fuzzy leaves, and the many prickles and spines give it a decidedly western look when an old wagon wheel or other country accent is set nearby. It may take all summer to get this annual to bloom in the cool climate closer to the coast, but farther east, where the soil is sandy and the sun is hot, prickly poppy can make quite a point.

PLANTING

Seeding: Direct sow in spring; indoors a few weeks earlier.

Planting out: Once soil has warmed.

Spacing: 12–16" (30–40 cm).

GROWING

Plant in a **full sun** location. **Good drainage** is essential for prickly poppies—**poor soil with grit** mixed in to enhance drainage is best. Prickly poppies like hot locations, therefore, a location against a wall facing south or west, where other plants tend to wilt, suits them nicely. Being quite large plants, they are most attractive mixed into the middle and back of a border. They also make effective barrier plants, under windows and along property lines, because the prickles can be somewhat unpleasant for people to walk through.

Prickly poppies don't like to have their roots disturbed. If direct sowing, plant them into their permanent locations outdoors or start them indoors in peat pots to avoid root disturbance when planting out.

ALTERNATE SPECIES

A. grandiflora has white or yellow flowers and the plant can grow as tall as 5' (1.5 m) in height and spread 12–18" (30–45 cm) wide.

GARDENING TIPS

Deadheading will keep the plants blooming and looking good.

PROBLEMS & PESTS

Downy mildew and bacterial leaf spot are possible problems.

The prickly nature of the poppy is a good burglar-deterrant under the windows of your house.

If anyone ventures to open the very prickly seedpods, they should not eat the seeds because they can cause stomach upset.

Rocket Larkspur
Annual Delphineum
Consolida ambigua (also called *Delphineum ajacis)*

Flower color: Blue, purple, pink or white.
Height: 12–48" (30–120 cm). **Spread:** 10–14" (25–35 cm).

*T*he explosive color of the dark blue rocket larkspur provides out-of-this-world color. The tall forms have delphinium-like flowers that are borne in single florets all the way up the stem, while the dwarf forms have multi-branching blooms. Both types give a vertical form to the flower that makes it perfect for partnering with the round blooms of daisies and geraniums. In my own garden, I use larkspur and other purple and blue cottage garden flowers around a wooden bench that has been stained sky blue. The gray leaves of lychnis and Russian sage provide a soothing foil to the bright blues and rich purples of the larkspur, and the whole effect is rather dreamlike—the colors are meant to relax.

Larkspur is also a sentimental favorite of many gardeners that remember it growing in their grandmother's garden.

PLANTING

Seeding: Indoors in mid-winter; direct sow in early or mid-spring.

Planting out: Mid-spring.

Spacing: 12" (30 cm).

GROWING

Rocket larkspur will do equally well in **full sun or light shade**. The soil should be **fertile, rich in organic matter** and **well drained**. Planting seeds in peat pots will prevent roots from being damaged when the plants are transplanted. Seeds started indoors may benefit from being chilled in the refrigerator for one week prior to sowing.

Plant groups of rocket larkspur in mixed borders or cottage gardens. Deadheading will keep these plants blooming well into fall. The tallest varieties may require staking to stay upright.

RECOMMENDED

'**Dwarf Blue Butterfly**' has compact plants that grow to 14" (35 cm) tall. Flowers are an intense deep blue.

Dwarf Rocket Series are available in many colors in plants that grow between 12–20" (30–50 cm) tall and 6–10" (15–25 cm) wide.

Giant Imperial Series also comes in many colors. The plants grow 24–36" (60–90 cm) tall and up to 14" (35 cm) wide.

GARDENING TIPS

Keep the roots of these plants cool and add a light mulch—dried grass clippings or shredded leaves work well. Don't mulch too closely to the base of the plant or it may develop crown rot.

PROBLEMS & PESTS

Slugs and snails are troublemakers to look out for. Powdery mildew and crown or root rot are avoidable if you water thoroughly, but not too often, and make sure the plants have good air circulation.

These flowers look good at the back of a border and make excellent cut flowers for arrangements.

Salvia
Sage
Salvia spp.

Flower color: Red, blue, purple, orange, pink or white.
Height: 8–36" (20–90 cm). **Spread:** 9–12" (23–30 cm).

*T*he bright red flower spikes of this sun lover won't disappoint if you appreciate fire-engine colors and lively form. The blue sage has a more soothing look, and it somewhat resembles lavender, with its gray leaves and thin flower spikes. Both types work well as components in mixed beds or planter gardens because their upright forms are perfect for the center of a large pot or the back of a narrow bed. Let white alyssum or trailing bacopa weave some contrasting white at the feet of the salvia and accent the scene with colorful coleus or zinnias for a summer garden of brightly hued blooms. Salvia also looks at home in formal gardens where its tidy, upright form looks great alongside a neatly trimmed boxwood hedge or along the edge of a crisply manicured lawn.

PLANTING

Seeding: Indoors in mid-winter; direct sow in spring.

Planting out: After last frost.

Spacing: 10" (25 cm).

GROWING

All sages prefer **full sun** but will tolerate light shade. The soil should be **moist** and **well drained** and of **average to rich fertility,** with **lots of organic matter**. All these sages are useful planted in groups in beds and borders as well as containers. When cut, the flowers are long lasting for arrangements.

RECOMMENDED

S. coccinea (Texas sage) has dark pink flowers on plants reaching 24–30" (60–75 cm) tall. **'Coral Nymph'** has delicate, coral pink flowers on compact plants reaching 18" (45 cm) tall.

S. farinacea (blue sage; mealy cup sage) has bright blue flowers clustered along stems powdered with silver. This flower is also available in

'Coral Nymph'

white. A popular cultivar of *S. farinacea* is **'Victoria,'** with silvery foliage that makes it a beautiful addition to cut flower arrangements.

S. splendens (salvia; scarlet sage) is known for its spikes of bright red, tubular flowers. Recently, cultivars have become available in white, pink, purple and orange.

S. viridis (annual clary sage) is grown for its colorful bracts and not its flowers. **'Claryssa'** grows 18" (45 cm) tall and has bracts in pink, purple, blue or white (photo on p. 202).

S. splendens

GARDENING TIPS

To keep plants producing flowers, water often and fertilize monthly.

PROBLEMS & PESTS

Seedlings are prone to damping-off. Aphids and a few fungus problems may occur.

S. viridus has been used externally to relieve sore gums. It has also been used as snuff and to flavor beers and wines.

S. farinacea

Scabiosa
Pincushion Flower
Scabiosa atropurpurea

Flower color: Purple, blue, pink or white.
Height: 12–36" (30–90 cm). **Spread:** Up to 15" (38 cm).

*T*he deep maroon and pink blossoms of the pincushion scabiosa have protruding stamens that look like pins. The details of the form make this flower one you'll be happy to pluck and bring indoors. It also has a sweet fragrance that butterflies love and an easy-to-please personality that makes it a welcome guest in any garden. Contrast the rounded blooms of scabosia with spiky lavender or taller larkspur for a symphony of purple. Grow fluffy clouds of baby's breath or easy-to-dry stems of statice nearby for a cutting garden.

PLANTING

Seeding: Indoors in late winter; direct sow in mid-spring.

Planting out: After last frost.

Spacing: 12–15" (30–38 cm).

GROWING

Scabiosa grows best in **full sun**. The soil should be of **average to rich fertility, with plenty of organic matter** and be **well drained**. Scabiosa is useful in beds, borders and mixed containers. These flowers are also popular for use in fresh arrangements.

RECOMMENDED

Imperial Giants have a deep maroon color, as well as pink and rose shades.

ALTERNATE SPECIES

S. stellata has small, white flowers and is grown for its papery, orb-like seedpods. It grows 18" (45 cm) tall and spreads half as much.

Seedpods of S. stellata *dry in unusual globe shapes, which are useful for accents in dried arrangements. Pick* S. stellata *while still slightly green to keep dried seedpods from shattering.*

Imperial Giants

Snapdragon

Antirrhinum majus

Flower color: White, cream, yellow, orange, red, maroon, pink, or bicolored.
Height: 12–48" (30–120 cm) depending on variety.
Spread: 6–24" (15–60 cm) depending on variety.

Snapdragons are part of many gardeners typical childhood memories. Plant a row of these easy-to-please spiky flowers and introduce them to all the youngsters in your life. Squeezing the sides of the complex flowers makes them pop open like a dragon's mouth, and growing the yellow, pink and bronze blooms will make your garden resonate with all the charm of a picture-book painting. I love to see snapdragons growing in front of a picket fence, with rambling roses dangling overhead and soft clouds of pink and purple alyssum blooming at the dragon's feet.

Snapdragons may self sow, providing you with new offspring each year.

PLANTING

Seeding: Indoors in late winter; direct sow in spring.

Planting out: After last frost.

Spacing: 6–18" (15–45 cm), depending on variety.

GROWING

Snapdragons prefer **full sun** but will tolerate light or partial shade. The soil should be **fertile, rich in organic matter** and **well drained**. Snapdragons prefer a neutral or alkaline soil and will not perform as well in acidic soil. If your soil is very acidic, it may be best to choose the smaller snapdragon varieties and grow them in planters where it is easier to prepare the soil to their liking.

Sow seeds on surface and do not cover them, because they require light for germination.

Snapdragons are interesting and long lasting in fresh flower arrangements. The buds will continue to mature and open even after the spike is cut.

The height of the variety dictates the best place for the plant in the border—the shortest ones near the front and the tallest ones in the center or back of the border. The dwarf and medium height varieties can also be used in planters, and there is even a variety available that has a droopy habit that does well in a hanging basket.

Snapdragons are perennials grown as annuals, they can tolerate cold nights. and some may survive winter if left in place in fall. They tend not to do as well a second year, and it is usually better to start new plants each year.

RECOMMENDED

There are many cultivars available with new ones introduced each year. Snapdragons are grouped into three sizes; dwarf, medium and tall. The shortest or dwarf varieties grow up to 12" (30 cm) tall. Medium height snapdragons grow 12–24" (30–60 cm) tall. The tallest can grow 36–48" (90–120 cm) tall.

Lampion Series is a new and interesting cultivar, which is a trailing plant that cascades up to 36" (90 cm). It is a great plant for hanging baskets.

Not only do the flowers pop open when squeezed like a dragon's mouth, but the vibrant colors will glow like embers in your flowerbeds.

GARDENING TIPS

The tallest of the snapdragons will probably need to be staked. To encourage bushier growth, pinch the tips of the plants while they are young.

Cut off the flower spikes as they fade to promote further blooming and to prevent the plant from dying back before the end of the season. Spikes left at the end of the season may set seed that will sprout the following summer.

PROBLEMS & PESTS

There are several fungus pests that can cause problems for snapdragons. Snapdragon rust is the worst of them. There are resistant varieties available, and planting them in different parts of the garden each year can help prevent the problem. To prevent rust, do not wet foliage when watering.

Powdery mildew, fungal leaf spot, root rot, wilt and downy mildew are other possible fungus problems.

Aphids are sometimes a problem. They can be sprayed off with water.

Spider Flower
Cleome
Cleome hasslerana

Flower color: Pink, rose, violet or white.
Height: 36–72" (90–180 cm). **Spread:** 18–36" (45–90 cm).

*T*he most spectacular spread of *Cleome* I ever saw was blooming next to a large pond with exotic cannas and broad-leaved banana trees, which set off the unusual spider-like blooms. Tall but graceful, spider flower needs some lower flowers to provide bulk and support. Large drifts of daisies, clumps of ornamental grass or sturdy shrub roses work well. Use this tall, late summer bloomer in the middle of an island bed, as a background planting or to form a late summer screen.

PLANTING
Seeding: Indoors in late winter; direct sow in spring.

Planting out: After last frost.

Spacing: 18–30" (45–75 cm).

GROWING

Spider flower prefers **full sun** but tolerates partial shade. Any kind of soil will do fine. Mix in **plenty of organic matter** to help the soil retain moisture. These plants are drought-tolerant but will look and perform better if watered regularly but not excessively or the plants will become leggy.

Before planting, chill seeds overnight.

Mass plant spider flower in the center of an island bed with lower-growing plants around the edges to hide the leafless lower stems. It can also be planted in groups at the back of a border.

RECOMMENDED

'**Helen Campbell**' has white flowers.

Royal Queen Series have flowers in all colors. These flowers are available by color or as a mixture of all available colors. The varieties are named by their color, e.g., '**Rose Queen**,' '**Violet Queen**' and '**Cherry Queen**.' The varieties in this series are resistant to fading.

Royal Queen Series

GARDENING TIPS

Be careful when handling these plants, because they have nasty barbs along the stems.

Deadhead to prolong the blooming period. Deadheading will also prevent the prolific self-sowing that can happen with spider flower. Self-sown seedlings will start coming up almost as soon as the seeds hit the ground and can become invasive. Fortunately, the plants are very distinctive and can be quickly spotted poking up where they don't belong, making them easy to pull up while still young.

PROBLEMS & PESTS

Aphids may be a problem.

The flowers can be cut for fresh arrangements, although the plants have an unusual odor that is very noticeable up close.

Statice

Limonium sinuatum

Flower color: Blue, pink, white, yellow, orange, red or purple.
Height: 16–24" (40–60 cm); taller and shorter varieties available.
Spread: 12" (30 cm).

*E*njoy statice in a cutting garden with strawflowers, scabosia and baby's breath for dried floral arrangements. You can also enjoy statice as a fresh flower and the deep purple statice is especially attractive accenting a vase of yellow snapdragons or pink roses. One of the most beautiful weddings I ever attended used purple, lavender and blue statice to accent pink and white roses in all the bouquets and the table centerpiece. It was a charming country look but with a sophisticated air—and all the more personal because the bride's mother had grown all the statice herself in a patch of rocky soil along the sunny side of the house.

PLANTING

Seeding: Indoors in mid-winter; direct sow in spring.

Planting out: After last frost.

Spacing: 12" (30 cm).

GROWING

Statice prefer **full sun**. The soil should be of **poor or average fertility, light, sandy** and **well drained**. Germination is 14–21 days. When planting out, remember that these plants don't like having their roots disturbed, a good approach is to start them in peat pots. These plants are perennials that are grown as annuals.

RECOMMENDED

Petite Bouquet Series has compact, 12" (30 cm) plants, with flowers in all colors.

Sunburst Series has flowers in warm hues of orange, peach and rose.

GARDENING TIPS

The basal leaves of statice grow flat and in a circular motion similar to the habit of biennials. Because the stalk is sent up from the middle of the plant; close spacing is more attractive in the garden than the usual recommended spacing.

Cut statice for drying late in summer, once the white center has come out on the bloom. It's not necessary to hang statice upside-down to dry; simply stand the stalks in a vase with about one inch of water and they will dry quite nicely on thier own.

PROBLEMS & PESTS

Most problems can be avoided by providing a well-drained site and ensuring that there is good air circulation around the plants.

Statice make an interesting addition to any sunny border, particularly in informal gardens. They are frequently used in fresh and dried arrangements.

Stock

Matthiola spp.

Flower color: Pink, purple, red, rose or white.
Height: 8–36" (20–90 cm) tall. **Spread:** 12" (30 cm).

Illuminate a moonlit evening garden with strongly scented stock; add moonflower vine to scramble up a trellis nearby for additional moon-lit blooms and evening perfume. Stock makes a strong vertical point in the landscape and is a good background plant for mounds of daisies or for the colorful foliage of coleus, which can help hide the rather awkward stems. Florists love stock for its long vase life, and many a bride has carried white stock down the aisle in classic white bouquets.

PLANTING

Seeding: Indoors in mid-winter;
in mild winter climates, direct sow in fall.

Planting out: After last frost.

Spacing: 12" (30 cm).

GROWING

Stock prefers **full sun** but will tolerate partial shade. The soil should be of **average fertility**, have **lots of organic matter** worked in and be **moist** but **well drained**.

Seeds can be started indoors in mid-winter. Leave seeds uncovered, because they require light to germinate. Plant in spring for summer blooms. If you plant outdoors in fall, flowers will bloom in late winter and early spring.

Stocks can be used in mixed beds or in mass plantings. Night-scented stocks should be where their wonderful scent can be enjoyed in an evening—near windows that are left open, beside patios or along pathways. It is best to plant night-scented stocks with other plants because they tend to look wilted and bedraggled during the day, only to revive impressively at night.

RECOMMENDED

M. incana (stock) has many cultivar groups with new ones introduced each year. Its colors range from pink, purple, red, rose or white. The height can vary from 8–36" (20–90 cm), depending on the cultivar. A popular group is the **Cinderella Series**, which has fragrant, colorful flowers. The compact plants grow to about 10" (25 cm) tall.

M. longipetala ssp. *bicornis* (night-scented stock; evening-scented stock) has pink or purple flowers that fill the evening air with their scent. Plants grow 12–18" (30–45 cm) tall.

PROBLEMS & PESTS

Poorly drained soil and low air circulation may encourage root rot or other fungus problems. Slugs are attracted to young foliage.

M. incana

For cut flowers, cut and then crush the woody stems so they will draw water more easily.

M. incana

Strawflower
Everlasting • Golden Everlasting
Bracteantha bracteata (also called *Helichrysum bracteatum*)

Flower color: Yellow, red, orange, pink, white or purple.
Height: 12–36" (30–90 cm) or taller. **Spread:** 12–24" (30–60 cm).

*T*he dry soil in a sun-baked rockery held the most attractive stand of strawflowers I ever grew. They were the low-growing dwarfs that could spill over the rocks and still look tidy. Grow the taller varieties in a cutting garden or in an out-of-sight side garden, because the plants themselves are a bit gawky. This plant is grown for its easily dried flowers. A good tip if you want to use the papery dried blossoms in an arrangement is to save just the flowerheads, not the weak stems. Insert a florist's wire into the bottom of the flowerhead until it sticks out from the yellow center. Bend the tip of this wire down like a shepard's crook, and pull the wire back down into the flower until it disappears from view. Strawflowers are easy to attach to wreaths and wall displays with a hot glue gun.

PLANTING

Seeding: Indoors in early spring; direct sow after last frost.

Planting out: After last frost.

Spacing: 10–18" (25–45 cm).

GROWING

Strawflowers prefer to be planted in locations that receive **full sun**. The soil should be of **average fertility, sandy, moist** and **well drained**. These plants are drought-tolerant. Sow seeds uncovered because they require light to germinate.

Include strawflowers in mixed beds, borders and containers. The lowest growing varieties are useful edging plants.

RECOMMENDED

Bikini Series has large, colorful flowers on compact plants that grow to about 12" (30 cm) tall.

Pastel Mixed has smaller flowers in soft tones that blend in well with other colors.

GARDENING TIPS

Taller varieties may require staking.

PROBLEMS & PESTS

Strawflowers are susceptible to downy mildew.

The most popular use of strawflower is for fresh or dried flower arrangements. To dry, hang fully opened flowers upside down in bunches.

Summer Forget-Me-Not

Cape Forget-Me-Not
Anchusa capensis

Flower color: Blue. **Height:** Up to 18" (45 cm); dwarf varieties available.
Spread: Up to about 12" (30 cm), depending on variety.

These intense blue blossoms are gorgeous on their own but when combined with clear yellow marigolds and deep red petunias the colors will shout with saturated intensity. Summer forget-me-not is not picky about soil, so it does well along a woodland path in full sun. New gardeners that haven't had the chance to improve the soil but still want lots of color will enjoy growing this adaptable annual. It can be used as a companion to early blooming flowers because it will mature later in the summer, filling in the beds with fresh color when spring bloomers have faded.

PLANTING

Seeding: Indoors in early winter; direct sow in fall.

Planting out: After last frost.

Spacing: 10–12" (25–30 cm).

GROWING

This plant grows best in a location that gets **full sun** but is not too hot. The soil should be **poor or average** and **well drained**. Starting seeds indoors in early winter will encourage more flowers. Seed is sown in fall to have flowers the following year. Chill seed one week before planting.

The larger varieties are most attractive mixed with other plants in a border. The smaller varieties can be mass planted together to create a sea of blue in a border. Use these flowers as a border filler. Dwarf varieties may need to be planted closer together than other varieties of summer forget-me-not. Summer forget-me-not is biennial but is grown as an annual.

RECOMMENDED

'Blue Angel' has intense blue flowers. These compact plants grow to 9" (23 cm) tall.

'Blue Heaven' has plants that grow 18–24" (45–60 cm) tall and masses of abundant blue flowers.

'Dawn' has blue, pink or white flowers. The plants grow 18" (45 cm) tall.

GARDENING TIPS

Trimming the plants back as they finish blooming will encourage them to keep on flowering throughout summer.

PROBLEMS & PESTS

Summer forget-me-not has occasional problems with cutworms and vine weevil larvae.

This plant originated in South Africa from the Cape of Good Hope, which is where the name cape forget-me-not was derived.

Sunflower

Helianthus spp.

Flower color: Most commonly yellow but also orange, red, brown or cream; typically with brown, purple or rusty red centers.
Height: Dwarf varieties, 24" (60 cm); giants up to 15' (4.5 m).
Spread: 12–24" (30–60 cm).

A weathered barn or tall garden shed is the perfect backdrop for a stand of sunflowers to blaze across. A display of sunflowers celebrates a late summer day in the country and has inspired artists as well as children as a favoured muse in artwork. Plant a row in the vegetable garden behind the tall stalks of corn, or use the lower varieties as a hedge along a split-rail fence. Tall companion plants such as spider flower or early summer bloomers such as foxgloves make good partners for the autumn blooms of sunflower. Sunflowers can also be used as cut flowers if you harvest them when the petals are open but the centers are still tight. Carefree gardeners can let sunflowers ripen and go to seed right in the garden to have new blooms the following summer.

PLANTING

Seeding: Indoors in late winter; direct sow in spring.

Planting out: After last frost.

Spacing: 12–24" (30–60 cm).

GROWING

Sunflowers grow best in **full sun**. The soil should be of **average fertility, humus-rich, moist and well drained**. The tallest varieties will need staking. The lower-growing varieties can be used in beds and borders. The tall varieties make good screens and temporary hedges or at the backs of borders.

Sunflowers are very popular with children and make excellent plants for them to grow. The seeds are big and easy to handle and they germinate quickly. The plants grow continually upwards and their progress can be measured until the flower finally appears on top of the tall plant. If planted along the wall of a two-storey house, the progress can be observed from above as well as below, making the flowers easy to see.

Sunflowers are grown as a crop seed for roasting, snacking or baking or for producing oil or flour.

The seeds are edible and attract birds. Use gray-seeded varieties for eating.

RECOMMENDED

H. annuus (common sunflower) is considered a fairly weedy plant, but the development of many new cultivars has revived the use of this plant in the garden. **'Music Box'** grows about 30" (75 cm) tall and has flowers in all colors, including some bicolors. **'Teddy Bear'** has fuzzy-looking, double flowers on plants 24–36" (60–90 cm) tall.

H. giganteus (giant sunflower) has bright yellow flowers 12" (30 cm) across. The plants grow 10' (3 m) or taller.

GARDENING TIPS

Birds will flock to the ripening seedheads of your sunflowers, quickly plucking clean the tightly packed seeds. If you plan on keeping the seeds to eat yourself you will have to place a mesh net, the sort used to keep birds out of cherry trees, around the flowerheads until the seeds ripen. This is can be a bit of a nuisance and doesn't look too great; most gardeners leave the flowers to the birds and buy seeds for personal eating.

PROBLEMS & PESTS

Powdery mildew may affect these plants.

Swan River Daisy

Brachycome iberidifolia

Flower color: Blue or pink (usually with purple hue); white with yellow centers.
Height: 8–18" (20–45 cm). **Spread:** Equal to or slightly greater than height.

I was endeared to the swan river daisy one summer when months of rain and cool weather melted the coleus and put the geraniums and petunias in a funk, causing many gardeners to throw in the trowel. The only bright spots in beds and pots was these long-blooming, tiny daisies, which continued to perform until the first week of December. The tiny blooms almost hide the ferny, green foliage on this finely textured annual, but the best trait is the long blooming time—this plant buds up and shows color in spring and doesn't stop until the first hard frost of winter. If you garden where the summers are cool, this solid bloomer will be an enduring performer for six months or more. Pair it with zinnias and begonias in container gardens, use it as a filler plant in moss baskets, or use it as a blooming groundcover with lysimachia. This frost-tolerant plant gives you long-lasting, dependable color.

PLANTING

Seeding: Indoors in late winter; direct-sow in mid-spring.

Planting out: Early spring.

Spacing: 12" (30 cm).

GROWING

Swan River Daisy prefers **full sun** but can benefit from light shade in the afternoon to prevent the plant from over-heating. The soil should be **fertile** and **well drained**. Allow the soil to dry between waterings.

Plant out early because cool spring weather encourages compact and sturdy growth. This plant is frost-tolerant and tends to die back if summer gets too hot. Cut it back if it begins to fade, and don't plant it in hot areas of the garden. A wall facing south or west is typically the hottest.

These versatile plants are useful for edging beds, in rock gardens, as well as in mixed containers and hanging baskets.

RECOMMENDED

'**Moonlight**' has white flowers with yellow eyes.

Splendor Series has dark-centered flowers in pink, purple or white.

'**Sunburst**' spreads quickly and has small, yellow to cream flowers.

GARDENING TIPS

Plant swan river daisy with plants that take longer to grow in. As swan river daisy is fading in July, the companions will be filling in and beginning to flower.

PROBLEMS & PESTS

A few problems, occasionally aphids, slugs or snails, will cause some trouble for this plant.

The flowers are fragrant and long lasting when cut for arrangments.

Sweet Alyssum

Lobularia maritima

Flower color: Pink, purple or white.
Height: 3–12" (8–30 cm). **Spread:** 6–24" (15–60 cm).

*I*n a brick courtyard, in the partly shaded front yard, blooms a stand of white sweet alyssum. These flowers are a testimony to the few plants I added to the border over a decade ago. Reseeding themselves in cracks and crevasses, eventually the lavender and purples will reseed to the original white color, which is the most fragrant variety. Sweet alyssum makes a lovely carpet of blooms to weave throughout a formal rose garden and also makes a great unifying plant to knit together different forms in the perennial garden.

PLANTING

Seeding: Indoors in late winter; direct sow in spring.

Planting out: Once soil has warmed.

Spacing: 8–12" (20–30 cm).

GROWING

Sweet alyssum prefers **full sun** but will tolerate light shade. Soil with **average fertility** is preferred but poor soil is tolerated. The soil should, in either case, be **well drained**. Use sweet alyssum in rock gardens, rock walls, between paving stones, along the edges of beds and borders or in mixed containers.

These plants dislike having their roots disturbed, a good approach to starting them indoors is to use peat pots or pellets.

Wonderland Series

RECOMMENDED

'Carpet of Snow' has pure white flowers on low, spreading, 3–4" (8–10 cm) tall plants.

'Oriental Night' has dark purple flowers on plants that spread to 8" (20 cm) wide.

Wonderland Series has a mix of all colors on compact plants.

GARDENING TIPS

Trimming this plant back occasionally over summer will keep it flowering and looking good.

Leave plant to sit out all winter. In spring remove last year's plant to expose self-sown seedlings below.

PROBLEMS & PESTS

Sweet alyssum rarely has any problems, but sometimes it battles downy mildew and slugs.

The sweetness of alyssum refers to its lovely fragrant flowers.

Sweet Pea

Lathyrus odoratus

Flower color: Pink, red, purple, lavender, blue, salmon, pale yellow, peach, white or bicolored. **Height:** Up to 6' (1.8 m); bush varieties, to about 12" (30 cm). **Spread:** 6–12" (15–30 cm).

No other flowers seem to bring out the emotions in people like sweetpeas. A vase of freshly cut blooms on a desk in an office will cause perfect strangers to stop and indulge in the fragrance from the gardens of their childhoods. Sweet peas are not the easiest annual to grow because they require cool weather and rich, well-worked soil, but successful sweet pea gardeners have the joy of creating lovely bouquets that warm hearts. Pastel or bicolors tint the puffy blooms, and the soft texture and rounded forms of the flowers have an instantly soothing effect, even without the fragrance. Plant sweet peas in the vegetable garden alongside the regular garden peas, or grow a heritage garden of old-fashioned plants that your grandmother loved, such as stock, violas, heliotrope and sweet peas.

PLANTING

Seeding: Direct sow in early spring.

Spacing: 6–12" (15–30 cm).

GROWING

Sweet peas prefer **full sun** but tolerate light shade. The soil should be **fertile, high in organic matter, moist** and **well drained**. Plants will tolerate light frost. Soak seeds in water for 24 hours before planting them, or nick them with a nail file.

Planting a second crop of sweet peas about a month after the first one will ensure a longer blooming period. A sowing in late summer will provide blooms in fall and early winter.

Sweet peas will grow up poles, trellises, fences or over rocks. The low-growing varieties will form low, shrubby mounds. An excellent way to provide privacy and hide a chain-link fence is to grow sweet peas up it.

Sweet peas are atractive and long lasting as cut flowers. Cutting sweet pea flowers encourages more blooms. Deadhead all spent blooms.

RECOMMENDED

There are many cultivars of sweet peas available.

Bijou Series is a popular heat-resistant variety that grows 18" (45 cm) tall, with an equal spread. It needs no support to grow.

Bouquet Mixed is a tall, climbing variety.

Supersnoop Series is a sturdy bush type that needs no support. It is fragrant with long stems. Pinch its tips to encourage low growth.

GARDENING TIPS

Avoid planting sweet peas in the same location two years in a row. It helps prevent some diseases from afflicting your sweet peas.

Fertilize very lightly during flowering season.

PROBLEMS & PESTS

Slugs and snail may be problems on the foliage of young plants. Root rot, mildew, rust and leaf spot may also afflict sweet peas occasionally.

Verbena
Garden Verbena
Verbena x *hybrida*

Flower color: Red, pink, purple, blue or white; usually with white centers.
Height: 8–18" (20–45 cm). **Spread:** Up to 20" (50 cm).

Think of verbena as the blooming ivy plant. It spreads in ground-hugging fashion and will drip from baskets and pots with rounded clusters of blooms in bright colors or soothing peachy orange tones. This annual demands dry, well-drained soil, so it is best grown on a sunny mound to avoid problems. The most attractive display with verbena I've seen was in a high school parking lot. A median strip was planted with low-growing, indestructible junipers—notorious for sucking moisture out of the soil—with waves of bright pink and lavender blue verbena blooming between the evergreens.

PLANTING

Seeding: Indoors in mid-winter.

Planting out: After last frost.

Spacing: 18" (45 cm).

GROWING

Verbena grows best in **full sun**. The soil should be **fertile** and **very well drained**. The bright colors and tolerance of dry locations make verbena popular in beds, borders, rock gardens, rock walls, containers and hanging baskets.

Chill seeds one week before sowing. Moisten the soil before sowing seeds. Do not cover the seeds with soil. Place entire seed tray or pots in darkness, or cover with newspaper or black plastic until seeds germinate. Only water seeds if soil becomes very dry. Once seeds germinate, they can be moved into the light.

Annual verbena makes quite a show dangling from window boxes, and it is a good substitute for ivy geraniums where the sun is hot and the overhang of a roof line keeps the soil and foliage of these mildew-prone plants dry.

RECOMMENDED

'Peaches and Cream' has flowers that open to a soft peach color and fade to white. The plants are spreading in habit.

Romance Series has red, pink, purple or white flowers. They grow to 8–10" (20–25 cm) tall.

ALTERNATE SPECIES

V. canadensis **'Homestead Purple'** is a very vigorous plant, which may come back the following spring in mild winter areas.

GARDENING TIPS

Pinch back young plants for bushy growth.

PROBLEMS & PESTS

Aphids, whiteflies, slugs and snails may be troublesome. Fungus can be a problem, but it can be avoided by making sure there is good air circulation around the plant and that the soil is well drained. This plant is susceptible to rot in wet climates.

For fall blooms, cut back the plants to half their size in midsummer.

Romance Series

Viola

Viola spp.

Flower color: Blue, purple, red, orange, yellow, pink, white or multicolored.
Height: 3–9" (8–23 cm). **Spread:** 6–12" (15–30 cm).

Viola is a cottage garden staple, and the most-loved viola called Johnny-jump-up makes a dazzling display each spring in my gravel driveway, having escaped years ago from a rock garden. I shear the plants back once the heat of summer arrives, but often in fall new seedlings will begin a second flush of bloom. Let random seeds spout in such unlikely spots as between evergreen shrubs and in the cracks of sidewalks. I also transplant young budded plants to pots of spring bulbs just before they both bloom. The lower growing violas provide a skirt of delicate flowers around the ankles of taller blooming tulips and daffodils.

PLANTING

Seeding: Indoors in early winter or mid-summer.

Planting out: Early spring or early fall.

Spacing: 6" (15 cm).

GROWING

Violas prefer **full sun** but will tolerate partial shade. The soil should be **fertile, moist** and **well drained**.

If you sow seeds indoors in early winter, spring flowers will bloom, while sowing indoors in mid-summer will provide fall and early winter blooms. It is not recommended to direct sow violas. Germination will be greater if seeds are kept in darkness until they germinate. Dark closets, dark plastic or layers of newspaper will provide enough darkness.

V. × wittrockiana

Johnny-jump-up gets its name from the fact that it reseeds profusely and tends to show up in the most unlikely places. This small plant has an affinity for lawns and just about any nook or cranny it can find to grow in.

V. × wittrockiana

V. tricolor

In milder climates, violas do well when the weather is cooler. They may even die back completely in summer. Violas may rejuvenate in fall, but it is often easier to plant new ones in fall and not take up garden space with plants that don't look good.

Violas can be used in beds and borders, and they are popular for mixing in with spring-flowering bulbs. They can also be grown in containers. The larger flowering pansy plants are preferred for early spring color amongst the primroses in garden beds.

RECOMMENDED

V. tricolor (Johnny-jump-up) is a popular species. The flowers are purple, white and yellow, usually in combination, although several varieties have flowers in a single color, often purple. This plant will thrive in gravel.

V. x wittrockiana (pansy) comes in blue, purple, red, orange, yellow, pink, white and often multicolored or with face-like markings. **Watercolor Series** is a newer group of cultivars with flowers in delicate pastel shades. **Joker Series** has bi- or multicolored flowers with distinctive face marking. It comes in all colors.

PROBLEMS & PESTS

Slugs and snails can be problematic. There are also some fungus problems that can be avoided through good air circulation and good drainage.

Collect short vases, such as perfume bottles with narrow necks, for displaying the cut flowers of pansies and violets. The more you pick, the more blooms you will get. These flowers are also one of the easiest to press between sheets of wax paper, weighted down with stacks of books.

V. x wittrockiana

Wishbone Flower

Torenia fournieri

Flower color: Purple, pink, blue or white;
often bicolored with yellow spot on lower petal.
Height: Up to 12" (30 cm). **Spread:** 6–12" (15–30 cm).

*I*n a cool, moist, shaded section of my garden, few annuals bloom well, and I thought I would have to settle with ferns to fill the bed. Then I discovered wishbone flower, and I couldn't wish for a better shade garden flower. The blooms resemble small gloxinias, and their low growth makes them perfect for the front of my border. The rich purple and blue blossoms are accented with white, so adding to the bed shade-tolerant lobelia and soft pink, fibrous begonias creates a rich tapestry of color that thrives when summer is slow to start and days are cool and moist.

PLANTING

Seeding: Indoors in mid-winter.

Planting out: After last frost.

Spacing: 8" (20 cm).

GROWING

Wishbone flower prefers **light shade**, but it will tolerate partial to full shade. The soil should be **fertile, light, rich in organic matter** and **moist**. This plant needs to be watered regularly.

Don't cover seeds when planting, because they need light to germinate.

Wishbone flower can be massed in a bed or border, used as an edging plant, and mixed with other plants in containers or hanging baskets. It can also be grown as a houseplant. The appearance of this plant is very soothing and subtle, and it blends well in a shade garden.

RECOMMENDED

Clown Series has compact plants, 6–8" (15–20 cm) tall, with early blooms in all colors.

PROBLEMS & PESTS

Some fungus problems may develop if the plant is growing in soil that is too wet. Although it likes moist soil, it also requires good air circulation around its roots.

In fall, dig up the plants and enjoy them indoors as blooming houseplants.

Zinnia
Zinnia elegans

Flower color: Red, yellow, green, purple, orange, pink or white.
Height: 6–36" (15–90 cm), depending on variety. **Spread:** 12" (30 cm).

*F*or a rainbow of blooms, fill a brick planter or pot on a sunny patio with zinnias and you'll have armloads of cut flowers until the first frost. You don't even have to buy transplants of this easy-to-grow annual, just sprinkle the seeds on top of the soil in your pots or throughout the beds and see what pops up. The dwarf zinnias are perfect as edging plants for tidy gardens, because their upright form keeps them in their place and unlike other low growers, they won't be creeping and spreading all over the pathway.

PLANTING

Seeding: Indoors in late winter; direct sow after last frost.

Planting out: After last frost.

Spacing: 6–12" (15–30 cm).

GROWING

Zinnias grow best in **full sun**. The soil should be **fertile, rich in organic matter, moist** and **well drained**. Zinnias are useful in beds and borders, in containers and in cutting gardens. The dwarf varieties can be used as edging plants. They are great for fall color. Combine the rounded form of the zinnia flower with the spiky blooms of sun-loving salvia, or use the taller varieties in front of sunflowers in fertile soil in a dry, sunny location they both will love. When starting the seeds indoors, plant them in individual peat pots.

Zinnias make excellent, long-lasting cut flowers for fresh arrangements.

Cactus-flowered zinnia

RECOMMENDED

Zinnia flowers come in several forms including single, double and cactus flowered. On a cactus-flowered bloom the petals appear to be rolled into tubes like the quills of a cactus.

'California Giants' have large, double flowers in a wide range of colors. Their bushy plants grow to 36" (90 cm) tall.

'Peter Pan' grows up to 12" (30 cm) tall, but it starts blooming early at 6" (15 cm), with flowers in mixed colors.

Thumbelina Series has small flowers in all colors on dwarf, 6" (15 cm), weather-resistant plants.

GARDENING TIPS

Deadheading is required to keep zinnias flowering and looking their best.

To keep mildew from the leaves, do not wet foliage when you water.

PROBLEMS & PESTS

Zinnias are prone to mildew and other fungus problems. Good air circulation and drainage is essential to keep them fungus free.

Though zinnias are quite drought-tolerant, they will grow best if watered thoroughly when their soil dries out. Use a soaker hose to avoid wetting the leaves.

Quick Reference Chart
HEIGHT LEGEND Low: < 12" (30 cm) • Medium: 12–24" (30–60 cm) • Tall: > 24" (60 cm)

SPECIES by Common Name	COLOR									SOWING		HEIGHT		
	White	Pink	Red	Orange	Yellow	Blue	Purple	Green	Foliage	Indoors	Direct	Low	Medium	Tall
African Daisy	✿	✿	✿	✿	✿					✿	✿		✿	
Ageratum	✿	✿				✿	✿			✿	✿	✿	✿	
Amaranth			✿		✿			✿	✿		✿			✿
Baby's Breath	✿	✿	✿				✿				✿		✿	
Bachelor's Buttons	✿	✿	✿			✿	✿			✿	✿	✿	✿	✿
Bacopa	✿	✿					✿					✿		
Begonia	✿	✿	✿	✿	✿				✿	✿		✿	✿	
Bells-of-Ireland								✿		✿	✿			✿
Black-eyed-Susan			✿	✿	✿					✿	✿		✿	✿
Black-eyed Susan Vine	✿			✿	✿					✿	✿			✿
Blanket Flower			✿	✿	✿					✿	✿	✿	✿	
Blue Lace Flower	✿					✿	✿				✿		✿	
Blue Marguerite	✿					✿				✿			✿	
Browallia	✿					✿	✿			✿		✿	✿	
Butterfly Flower		✿	✿		✿		✿			✿		✿	✿	
Calendula	✿			✿	✿						✿		✿	✿
California Poppy	✿	✿	✿	✿	✿		✿				✿		✿	
Candytuft	✿	✿	✿				✿				✿	✿	✿	
Canturbury Bells	✿	✿				✿	✿			✿			✿	✿
Cape Marigold	✿	✿		✿	✿					✿	✿		✿	
China Aster	✿	✿	✿	✿	✿	✿	✿			✿	✿		✿	✿
Chrysanthemum	✿		✿		✿		✿				✿		✿	
Cockscomb		✿	✿	✿	✿		✿					✿	✿	✿
Coleus							✿		✿	✿		✿	✿	✿
Coreopsis			✿	✿	✿						✿	✿		✿
Cosmos	✿	✿	✿	✿	✿					✿	✿		✿	✿
Creeping Zinnia				✿	✿						✿	✿		

Quick Reference Chart

SPECIES by Common Name

Hardy	Half-hardy	Tender	Sun	Part Shade	Light Shade	Shade	Moist	Well Drained	Dry	Fertile	Average	Poor	Page Number	Species
		✿	✿				✿	✿			✿		42	African Daisy
		✿	✿	✿			✿	✿		✿			44	Ageratum
		✿	✿					✿			✿	✿	48	Amaranth
✿			✿					✿				✿	52	Baby's Breath
✿			✿				✿	✿	✿	✿	✿		54	Bachelor's Buttons
		✿	✿	✿			✿	✿			✿		56	Bacopa
		✿	✿	✿	✿	✿		✿		✿			58	Begonia
	✿		✿	✿				✿		✿	✿		62	Bells-of Ireland
	✿		✿	✿			✿			✿	✿		64	Black-eyed-Susan
		✿	✿	✿	✿		✿	✿		✿			68	Black-eyed-Susan Vine
✿			✿						✿		✿		70	Blanket Flower
✿			✿					✿			✿		72	Blue Lace Flower
	✿		✿					✿			✿		74	Blue Marguerite
		✿		✿	✿	✿		✿		✿			76	Browallia
		✿	✿				✿	✿		✿			78	Butterfly Flower
✿			✿	✿				✿			✿		80	Calendula
✿			✿	✿				✿	✿		✿	✿	82	California Poppy
✿			✿					✿			✿	✿	84	Candytuft
✿			✿	✿			✿	✿		✿			86	Canturbury Bells
		✿	✿					✿	✿	✿			88	Cape Marigold
		✿	✿	✿			✿			✿			90	China Aster
✿			✿	✿				✿			✿		92	Chrysanthemum
		✿	✿					✿		✿			94	Cockscomb
		✿	✿	✿	✿	✿	✿	✿		✿	✿		96	Coleus
✿			✿					✿	✿	✿	✿		100	Coreopsis
		✿	✿					✿	✿		✿	✿	102	Cosmos
		✿	✿						✿		✿		106	Creeping Zinnia

Quick Reference Chart
HEIGHT LEGEND Low: < 12" (30 cm) • Medium: 12–24" (30–60 cm) • Tall: > 24" (60 cm)

SPECIES by Common Name	White	Pink	Red	Orange	Yellow	Blue	Purple	Green	Foliage	Indoors	Direct	Low	Medium	Tall
				COLOR						SOWING		HEIGHT		
Cup Flower	✿					✿	✿			✿		✿		
Cup-and-saucer Vine	✿						✿			✿				✿
Dahlberg Daisy				✿	✿					✿	✿	✿		
Dahlia	✿	✿	✿	✿	✿		✿			✿		✿	✿	✿
Dusty Miller	✿				✿				✿	✿		✿	✿	
Dwarf Morning Glory	✿	✿				✿	✿			✿	✿	✿	✿	
Fan Flower						✿	✿			✿		✿		
Forget-me-not	✿	✿				✿					✿	✿		
Four-o'clock Flower	✿	✿	✿		✿					✿	✿		✿	✿
Fuchsia	✿	✿	✿				✿					✿	✿	✿
Gazania	✿	✿	✿	✿	✿					✿	✿	✿	✿	
Geranium	✿	✿	✿	✿			✿			✿		✿	✿	
Gerbera Daisy		✿	✿	✿	✿		✿			✿		✿	✿	
Globe Amaranth	✿	✿	✿				✿			✿		✿	✿	
Godetia	✿	✿	✿				✿				✿		✿	✿
Heliotrope	✿						✿			✿		✿	✿	
Impatiens	✿	✿	✿	✿			✿			✿		✿	✿	✿
Licorice Plant	✿				✿				✿	✿	✿		✿	✿
Livingstone Daisy	✿	✿	✿	✿	✿					✿	✿	✿		
Lobelia	✿	✿	✿			✿	✿			✿		✿		
Love-in-a-mist	✿	✿				✿	✿			✿	✿		✿	✿
Madagascar Periwinkle	✿	✿	✿				✿			✿		✿	✿	
Mallow	✿	✿	✿								✿			✿
Marigold			✿	✿	✿					✿	✿	✿	✿	✿
Mexican Sunflower			✿	✿	✿					✿	✿			✿
Million Bells	✿	✿		✿	✿		✿					✿		
Morning Glory	✿	✿				✿	✿			✿	✿			✿

Quick Reference Chart

Hardy	Half-hardy	Tender	Sun	Part Shade	Light Shade	Shade	Moist	Well Drained	Dry	Fertile	Average	Poor	Page Number	SPECIES by Common Name
	✿		✿	✿	✿		✿			✿			108	Cup Flower
		✿	✿					✿			✿		110	Cup-and-saucer Vine
✿			✿					✿			✿	✿	112	Dahlberg Daisy
		✿	✿				✿	✿		✿			114	Dahlia
	✿		✿		✿			✿			✿		118	Dusty Miller
		✿	✿					✿	✿		✿	✿	120	Dwarf Morning Gl;ory
		✿	✿		✿		✿	✿			✿		122	Fan Flower
✿				✿	✿		✿			✿			124	Forget-me-not
		✿	✿	✿				✿			✿	✿	126	Four-o'clock Flower
		✿	✿	✿	✿		✿	✿		✿			128	Fuchsia
		✿	✿	✿				✿	✿		✿	✿	132	Gazania
		✿	✿	✿				✿		✿			134	Geranium
	✿		✿	✿				✿			✿	✿	138	Gerbera Daisy
		✿	✿					✿			✿		140	Globe Amaranth
✿			✿		✿				✿		✿	✿	142	Godetia
		✿	✿				✿	✿		✿			144	Heliotrope
		✿		✿	✿	✿	✿			✿			146	Impatiens
✿			✿	✿				✿			✿	✿	150	Licorice plant
		✿	✿						✿		✿	✿	152	Livingstone Daisy
✿			✿	✿	✿		✿			✿			154	Lobelia
✿			✿					✿			✿		156	Love-in-a-mist
		✿	✿	✿			✿		✿	✿	✿	✿	158	Madagascar Periwinkle
✿			✿					✿			✿		160	Mallow
	✿		✿					✿	✿		✿		164	Marigold
		✿	✿						✿		✿	✿	168	Mexican Sunflower
	✿		✿				✿	✿		✿			170	Million Bells
		✿	✿					✿			✿	✿	172	Morning Glory

Quick Reference Chart
HEIGHT LEGEND Low: < 12" (30 cm) • Medium: 12–24" (30–60 cm) • Tall: > 24" (60 cm)

SPECIES by Common Name	White	Pink	Red	Orange	Yellow	Blue	Purple	Green	Foliage	Indoors	Direct	Low	Medium	Tall
Nasturtium	✿	✿	✿	✿	✿					✿	✿		✿	
Nicotiana	✿	✿	✿		✿		✿	✿		✿	✿		✿	✿
Painted-tongue		✿	✿	✿	✿		✿			✿			✿	
Petunia	✿	✿	✿		✿		✿			✿		✿	✿	
Phlox	✿	✿	✿		✿	✿	✿				✿	✿	✿	
Poppy	✿	✿	✿	✿	✿		✿				✿			✿
Portulaca	✿	✿	✿	✿	✿		✿			✿		✿		
Prairie Gentian	✿	✿			✿	✿	✿			✿		✿	✿	
Prickly Poppy	✿				✿		✿			✿	✿			✿
Rocket Larkspur	✿	✿				✿	✿			✿	✿		✿	✿
Salvia	✿	✿	✿	✿		✿	✿			✿	✿	✿	✿	✿
Scabiosa	✿	✿				✿	✿			✿	✿		✿	✿
Snapdragon	✿	✿	✿	✿	✿		✿			✿		✿	✿	✿
Spider Flower	✿	✿					✿			✿	✿			✿
Statice	✿	✿	✿	✿	✿	✿	✿			✿	✿		✿	✿
Stock	✿	✿	✿				✿				✿	✿	✿	✿
Strawflower	✿	✿	✿	✿	✿		✿			✿	✿		✿	✿
Summer Forget-me-not						✿				✿		✿	✿	
Sunflower	✿		✿	✿	✿						✿			✿
Swan River Daisy		✿				✿	✿			✿	✿	✿	✿	
Sweet Alyssum	✿	✿					✿			✿	✿	✿		
Sweet Pea	✿	✿	✿			✿	✿	✿			✿	✿		✿
Verbena	✿	✿	✿			✿	✿			✿		✿	✿	
Viola	✿	✿	✿	✿	✿	✿	✿			✿		✿		
Wishbone Flower	✿	✿				✿	✿			✿		✿		
Zinnia	✿	✿	✿	✿	✿			✿	✿	✿	✿	✿	✿	✿

Quick Reference Chart

Hardy	Half-hardy	Tender	Sun	Part Shade	Light Shade	Shade	Moist	Well Drained	Dry	Fertile	Average	Poor	Page Number	SPECIES by Common Name
		✿	✿	✿	✿			✿	✿		✿	✿	176	Nasturtium
		✿	✿	✿	✿		✿	✿		✿			180	Nicotiana
		✿	✿					✿		✿			182	Painted-tongue
	✿		✿					✿			✿	✿	184	Petunia
✿			✿				✿			✿			188	Phlox
✿			✿					✿		✿			190	Poppy
		✿	✿						✿			✿	194	Portulaca
	✿		✿	✿	✿			✿			✿		196	Prairie Gentian
	✿		✿					✿				✿	198	Prickly Poppy
✿			✿	✿	✿			✿		✿			200	Rocket Larkspur
	✿	✿	✿	✿	✿		✿	✿		✿	✿		202	Salvia
	✿		✿					✿		✿	✿		206	Scabiosa
	✿		✿	✿	✿			✿		✿			208	Snapdragon
	✿		✿	✿			✿		✿	✿	✿	✿	212	Spider Flower
		✿	✿					✿			✿	✿	214	Statice
✿			✿	✿			✿	✿		✿			216	Stock
	✿		✿				✿	✿	✿	✿			218	Strawflower
		✿	✿	✿				✿			✿	✿	220	Summer Forget-me-not
✿			✿				✿	✿		✿			222	Sunflower
	✿		✿	✿	✿			✿		✿			226	Swan River Daisy
✿			✿		✿			✿			✿	✿	228	Sweet Alyssum
✿			✿		✿		✿			✿			230	Sweet Pea
		✿	✿					✿	✿	✿			232	Verbena
✿			✿	✿	✿		✿			✿			234	Viola
		✿		✿	✿	✿	✿			✿			238	Wishbone Flower
		✿	✿					✿	✿	✿			240	Zinnia

Glossary

Acid soil: soil with a pH lower that 7.0

Alkaline soil: soil with a pH higher than 7.0

Annual: a plant that germinates, flowers, sets seed and dies in one growing season

Basal leaves: leaves that forms from the crown

Biennial: a plant that germinates and produces stems, roots and leaves in the first growing season; it flowers, sets seed and dies in the second growing season

Crown: the point at or just below soil level where the shoots join the roots

Cultivar: a plant cultivated for desirable characteristics, such as flower color, leaf variegation or disease resistance, that will pass on these characteristics by seed or vegetative propagation

Damping off: fungal disease causing seedlings to rot at soil level and topple over

Deadhead: to remove spent flowers to maintain attractiveness and encourage a longer blooming period

Disbud: to remove some flowerbuds in order to improve the size or quality of the remaining ones

Dormancy: a period, typically during unfavorable conditions, when a plant ceases growth activity

Double flower: a flower made up entirely of petals with few or no stamens, e.g., dahlia, p. 114 (see photo on opposite page)

Genus: a taxonomic grouping above species level; the first word of the scientific name

Hardy: describes a plant capable of surviving a fairly heavy frost; often intolerant of heat

Harden off: to gradually acclimatize plants that have been growing in a protective environment to a more harsh environment, e.g., plants started indoors being moved outdoors

Humus: decomposed, or decomposing, organic material in the soil

Hybrid: a cross breed, either naturally occurring or cultivated, between two or more distinct species within a genus or between closely related genera; the hybrid expresses features of each parent plant

Invasive: a plant that grows so vigorously that it overwhelms the plants that grow around it, sometimes spreading indefinitely

Neutral soil: soil with a pH of 7.0

Node: the area on a stem from which a leaf or new shoot grows

pH: the scale used to measure acidity or alkalinity; the pH of soil influences the availability of nutrients

Perennial: a plant that takes three or more years to complete its life cycle; a herbaceous perennials normally dies back to the ground over winter

Rhizome: a food-storing stem that grows horizontally at or just below soil level, from which new shoots may emerge

Root ball: a mass of soil and plant roots

Self-seeding: a plant that self-propagates from seed

Semi-hardy: describes a plant capable of surviving temperatures approaching freezing, but will be killed if they drop below freezing

Semi-double flower: a flower with petals that form two or three rings, e.g., calendula, p. 80 (see photo below)

Single flower: a flower with petals typically of four or five that form a single ring, e.g., cosmos, p. 102 (see photo below)

Species: group of plants that can interbreed with each other, but that have distinct individual characteristics

Straight species: the original species; from which cultivars and varieties are derived.

Tender: describes a plant incapable of surviving temperatures that approach freezing; often heat tolerant

True: when desirable characteristics are passed on from the parent plant to the seed-grown offspring; also called breeding true to type

Tuber: the thick section of a rhizome bearing nodes and buds

Variety: a naturally occurring variation or subdivision

Double flower

Single flower

Semi-double flower

Index